T0149248

Broken

A Thirst for Love

Larry Flemmings

WESTBOW
PRESS®
A DIVISION OF THOMAS NELSON
& ZONDERVAN

WestBow Press books may be ordered through booksellers or by contacting:

WestBow Press
A Division of Thomas Nelson & Zondervan
1663 Liberty Drive
Bloomington, IN 47403
www.westbowpress.com
1 (866) 928-1240

ISBN: 978-1-5127-2906-1 (sc)
ISBN: 978-1-5127-2907-8 (hc)
ISBN: 978-1-5127-2905-4 (e)

Library of Congress Control Number: 2016901699

Print information available on the last page.

WestBow Press rev. date: 2/18/2016

Dedication

I dedicate this book to my dad, John Flemmings, and the late Katie Flemmings, my mom. She was a person, with a lovely heart. I thank God that, later in life, I had the opportunity to get to know her, and I grew to love her. I'd never known a person like her before. Although I grew up without her and didn't meet her until later on in my life. I always had an idea of what a mother should or should not be, according to my personal understanding of this relationship. Getting to know my mother was something that I'd always wanted.

I wanted a mother who would give me hugs, love, and support. A mother who always inspired me was Claire Huxtable from *The Cosby Show*. Even though I never had the chance to receive my mother's love, I have always wondered what it would have felt like. Now that she has passed on, I will never know. I remember some things about her, like, when I was a child, waving good-bye to her with my eyes full of tears. It did not matter how much I cried, though, because the car kept going. I needed her to be there for me as a mother. It would be seventeen years before I saw her again. I needed her, just as all children need their mothers. Was that too much to ask? I needed my mom; I asked for nothing more and definitely nothing less. I needed the love of a mother so that I could, at least, feel the way that I thought others felt.

My father, on the other hand, claimed to love me. He showed his love with a switch, a belt, or whatever he could get his hands on. He had to let me know that he was not playing around because he had to get back to whatever it was he was doing. It was as if he would give me a fast and quick whooping that was the "Didn't I tell you? Didn't I? What did I say? Do what I told you to do!" type of chastising. I remember him laughing about it afterward, thinking it was funny and that he had done justice or something. Today my father's disciplinary methods would be considered child abuse.

I think that if you love someone and if chastisement needs to take place, you should not intentionally try to hurt him or her. I believe that if a person really loves someone, he or she should not have to chastise that person every time he or she does something wrong. My pops is a man who believes in respect. He literally believes in "spare the rod, spoil the child." That part of the Bible does not have to be taught because, if it was already being beat out of you, then why not pass it on! My dad just took things too serious.

I wish I had not been born in those days, because I had to suffer the heartaches and pains of being my father's son. I did not like it, but I think that because of it, it made me the person I am today. Even though I did not get a whole heap of beatings, I survived and am still here. Parents are not given a manual on how to be parents; however, I do know that in the Bible in the book of Hebrews 8:10 God said that He would put His teachings inside of us and He would write them on our hearts. He said that He would be our God, and we would be His people, so if He did all of that, then we should know right from wrong, because it is already in our hearts.

Synopsis

This book is the story of one man's struggle for perfection and how that struggle turned into failure, deceit, and destruction. For his life to be complete, after so many years of failures, he reached out to help enhance the lives of others. Life has many ups and downs. Struggles, challenging moments, and unbearable trials are parts of life. The struggles can be complicated sometimes, when you are doing the best you can just to feel a part of something. It is always hard when you are trying to be something that you are not; it is even harder trying to imitate the lives of others because of their outward appearance of perfection. While trying to wear someone else's shoes, you will often adopt a delusional mindset embedded with manipulative thoughts while always trying to be "the one."

The glory of a man's life is what he considers to be in his heart. A man's success is a mind-blowing experience when the beauty of life appears in the form of a woman (for God made the woman for the man). A woman's presence is what catches his attention and causes him to act differently because she throws him off course with her beauty. He sees that and misses out on the inner person, which is where the heart is and where the real person resides. Matthew 6:21 says, "For where your treasure is, there will your heart be also." The desire for outer beauty causes him to lose sight of what is on the inside. The Bible tells us that he who finds a wife finds a good thing. For instance the very appearance of a woman's' beauty can bring a man to his knees and to her beck and call.

Your heart does not lie. If you have ever had a gut feeling, believe it, because your intuition almost never lies to you. Most of the time, it reveals the truth. Every man desires are to have the love of his life should always be cautious and careful. Not all beauty is the same; beauty is but in the eye of the beholder. The way one person sees beauty is not the way another will see it. Remember: it was greed, selfishness, and beauty that caused Satan to lose his place in the heavenly realm.

In regards to having thoughts that pertain to the glory of life, things got worse and became the most obnoxious and nauseating part of life, and why? Because of the outer appearance. The beauty that is seen, most of the time, is what gets you trapped, caught up, and falling for what is seen versus the unseen. The outer appearance is appealing to the eyes, which overrule everything else. Without a doubt, valuing superficial beauty will cause you to fall into many temptations. It is a trap that lures people to the beauty of the outward parts while missing the big picture of things that are not there. One must be willing or capable of discerning things that will eventually put oneself in a state of desire for the outer appearance that does not specify what's on the inside.

Beauty is an expression that does not depict or define the reality of what is on the inside. The devil was heaven's beauty. Beauty does not define who or what a person is. Beauty is just appearance, but it simplifies and fails to verify who a person or what a thing is. It's just simply things that happen or will happen in life. For instance, cheetahs are beautiful animals. They, also, have charms. Otherwise, they would not have gotten any attention inwardly. Cheetahs are beasts, and their spots never change. Once a beast, always a beast, unless reformed. A moment of desire can become the awakening of life's structure and state of being; it is a change. It is the finale of a new beginning of accomplishments, and it is a wait that is well worth it.

If you are a person who has deep desires or thoughts, and if you reminisces and are anxious all the time, be careful, because it will get you caught up, trapped, and messed up, and it will leave you unable to think straight. The Bible tells us in Philippians 4:6 to be anxious for nothing, but in everything, by prayer and supplication with thanksgiving, let your request be made known. In my situation, I found that I still had not waited long enough for the right person to come along, and because I did not, it caused my life to become a living hell. I went through hell on earth, and I was on my way to hell hereafter. I was married and in hell at the same time, because every letter in hell was an indication of what I was going through, which was *h*ot, *e*vil, *l*onely, and *l*amenting, and this would continue throughout all eternity, with no chance of parole. Oh, my God, I thought, shaking my head. Once in hell, there is no chance of ever leaving. There will be no twenty years but doing half with good behavior. It is forever and ever that has no end.

I sought attractive outer appearances with hidden hearts, which made my loneliness, sadness, and need to be needed worse. Although I wanted and needed to be wanted and cared for, I still failed to make the right choices. So then I went from having to not having. I do not know what I really had or would have had if I had waited. You will find out and learn something, hopefully, as you read this ongoing message. Life can be tricky when we allow our selfish lusts to desire something that is not ours, but you will learn from your experiences, mistakes, and wants.

Moments

There are many things in life that are not perfect at all times. When things are going bad and it just seems like it is getting no better, you have to learn how to trust in the Lord and do well, according to his love, power, comfort, genuineness, and mighty acts of forgiveness. God has done so much for me. He has kept me from falling into temptation and giving in to thoughts and suggestions of ungodliness, such as rottenness, deceitfulness, wrongdoings, and accusations.

Personally, I give thanks to God for whom He has been and still is in my life. I love God with all of my heart, as David did and said in the Bible ("A man after God's own heart with a mind of never turning against Him lest he died"). I give my savior Jesus Christ honor and glory for all that He has done and is about to do in my life because He has blessed me throughout the good times, as well as the bad.

If it was not for the bad times in my life and His intervention in my life, I would have probably been lost and sleeping in my grave. I give God the praise and thanks for allowing me to be an influence in someone's life, for breaking bread with others, and for being a source of assistance in someone's relationship that seemed to be going downhill. I give God the praise for what He has done for me. I hope that someone will read and learn from my experiences. I've had to encounter so much in life in such a short time, so if I can be of help to those who might be going through something and need a little PUSH (meaning *Pray Until*

Something Happens), then this might truly help those of you who are going through hardships in your lives. Give a little. Live a little. A little here and a little there keeps on growing until it fully blossoms like a flower.

The same spark that initiated a relationship should last forever. Love does not and should not fade; it should always be there if it was there in the first place. The garden of Eden could have still been here, but sin caused it to disappear. It vanished because of greed, deception, carelessness, and because of the consumption of lustful desires. Many of us struggle with the dilemma of wants versus needs. We should be able to accept what we have and leave others alone. Just because it shines or glitters does not mean it's diamonds or gold. The devil can present some people as promising, but are they? Remember, the devil wears Prada. Satan looks like a sheep, but is he? No, he is a wolf in sheep's clothing, not the real thing.

The enemy always has something going on that will catch the attention of an onlooker who sees only a beautiful outer appearance. According to 2 Corinthians 11:14 (New American Standard), "No wonder; for even Satan disguises himself as an angel of light." This statement means he will let a person see what he or she wants to see as long as that person is looking at what he tempts him or her to look at or see. The enemy is conniving and deceiving. He gives no one a break, even when it seems good. The Bible lets us know that there is a way that may seem good or right to a man or woman, but in the end, the result is death and destruction. Do you want to know the truth or a lie?

I thank God for enabling me to go through life with the willpower to tackle any and all obstacles. I give honor to Him for my grandmother, who was there when I needed encouragement. I had no one other than her to guide me and teach me about life. My father was there, but my grandmother took care of me. My father was too busy, being in other places and making other children. He did not give me that fatherly affection that every child needs; instead, he pawned me off on his mother. I thank God for my mom, who has passed and gone on to be with the Lord, I pray and hope. I only say *hope* because of what the Bible says about going to heaven. John 3:13 tells us that there is no man—meaning nobody—who has ascended into heaven, but He that came down from heaven, even the Son of Man, which is in heaven. The Bible also goes on to tell us that to say that someone has gone to heaven is to bring Jesus down from heaven; it also tells us that to say that someone has gone to hell is to say that He has never ascended. However, the Bible does say that we would go into the bosom of Abraham, according to Luke 16:22–24 (King James Version AV), which reads, "And it came to pass, that the beggar died, and was carried by the angels into Abraham's bosom. The rich man also died and was buried: and in hell did he lift up his eyes, being in torments, sees Abraham afar off, and Lazarus in his bosom. And he cried and said, 'Father Abraham, have mercy on me, and send Lazarus that he may dip the tip of his finger in some water and cool my tongue, for I am tormented in this flame.'"

This scripture lets us know that there is fire in hell. Can you imagine? Abraham reminded the rich man of his lifestyle and said, "When you thought you had it going on and Lazarus had nothing, you gave him nothing of yours when he begged or asked. Don't worry. He is comfortable now, but as for you and because of what you did, you are now cast into the darkness upon darkness, in Hades, where there is no day, for the remainder of your existence is upon you and your home of internal and external fire in which walls are walls of darkness where there is 'weeping and gnashing of teeth'" (Matthew 8:12).

I thank God for putting the angel of deliverance in my path, for teaching me of the things to come, and for showing me the road to follow. God has blessed me with a grandmother to teach me and show me the way, according to God's standards. No thanks to my ever-so-loving father. Although I love him dearly and although he thought he could beat sense into me with a switch, gym belt, or a tractor fan belt, I don't think he knew the Bible as he should have. The Bible tells parents not to provoke their children to anger. According to Colossians 3:21, if you are going to punish him or her, let it be for a good reason and not just because you can or you are the parent who believes in "do as I say and not as I do." Children have rights as well. Parents may choose to discipline their children in the same ways they were disciplined when they were growing up because they know no other way. Even if they were beaten while tied up in a croaker sack as children, they might use the same harsh punishment on their children. Children do not come with a parenting manual; it's a learning experience. Parenting involves a superior responsibility in which we are all capable; however, not all are successful or engaged in the vital task. My mother was not around, for whatever reason, to take care of my siblings who were conceived in her womb or me.

My pops thought that taking care of his responsibilities meant whipping the problems out of my siblings and me every time something did not sit right with him. My dad thought it was the thing to do; instead, it drove me away. The chastisement I had to endure from him seemed wrong at the time, and it was, but I think it is what kept me out of trouble. I also say that no one should have to endure severe physical punishment from anyone; whether they are your parent or not, it doesn't matter.

I loved my mom, even though she was not there for me. I still hope to have the pleasure of finally meeting her. I discovered that I had an angel on Earth when my brother came to Georgia and provided me with her number. I had always wanted to hear my mother's voice. Hearing her first few words just blew me away because her voice was like the voice of an angel. Just hearing her voice influenced my life greatly. Her voice gave me hope. It gave me life. I really wanted to meet her one day to see what it would be like to be in her presence, knowing that she was all mine. My mama.

I felt love, joy, peace, and happiness when I was in the presence of a real *mother mama*. What is a mother mama? A mother is a woman who gives birth. A mama is a woman who takes care of and raises her children. Therefore, a mother mama is someone who does both—biologically gives birth and, also, nurtures her children and provides the things they need. A mother mama is much more than a biological ability or the duties of a mammy or nanny who takes care of others' children while leaving her own to suffer.

It was not easy. I had to go through some trials and tribulations to get to the place I needed to be. At times, I thought I would not make it, but I got there. God's will allowed me to go through some obstacles, not that I am happy or glad to have gone through them, but He allowed it, covered it, and kept me, and He has not let anything happen to me that I could not bear or handle. He has guided me and allowed me to get to know the person I have always wondered about—my mama. I thank God for delivering me, because if I had not gone through anything, I would not have anything to be thankful to Him for.

I know that if it were not for God bringing my brother and my grandmother together, it probably would have killed the hope of ever seeing my mother. My life today would be headed in an entirely different direction, which probably would have had me in a state of not giving him the praises and having the love for his people that I do now. I have gone through some things in my life that if I had to do them all over again, I probably would seriously have to say, "When hell freezes over," because going through that kind of agony and frustration again would be the worst joke of the century!

It is impossible to please God without having the spirit of truth within you. The things a person goes through make him or her strong or weak. A person who does not seem to go through anything needs to check himself or herself, and if he or she doesn't find anything wrong within, then that person is probably already halfway home, and there is nothing else the accuser of the brethren has to do. This attitude is called self-righteousness or self-indulgence. The devil will wait for the recovery of this person's misunderstandings. He will be your only keeper as your home awaits you, with its arms open to receive its prize—you. A person's wicked ways give the devil honor and pleasure, to greet the ear that once heard the word of god, and closed up your heart of compassion which is the way to the Gods heart.

Isaiah 5:14 (AV) reads: "Therefore hell hath enlarged herself, and opened up her mouth without measure: with their glory, and their multitude, and their pomp, and he that rejoices, shall descend into it."

Even though it was rough to have endured many painful experiences, it was only for me to go through and nobody else. Had it been anybody else, maybe even yourself, a friend, or someone else close to you, he or she probably would have taken his or her own life. God said in His word that He would not put any more on us than we could bear. A prime example of this is in 1 Corinthians 10:13 (AV): "There hath no temptation taken you but such as common to man: but God *is* faithful, who will not suffer you to be tempted above that ye are able; but will with temptations also make a way to escape, that ye may be able to bear *it.*"

God will fix whatever is broken, and He will fight your battles, but only if you believe that He rewards those who diligently seek Him. It is impossible to please God if there is no belief, faith, or trust in Him. Sometimes we need to know whom we put our faith and our trust in. It should not have to be for a particular reason. It is because of what we think or feel about things. God still loves us, despite whatever we may be going through, because He cares for us with an unconditional heart. He reigns over the just as well as the unjust. He gives us all a chance, the righteous as well as the not-so-righteous. As intelligent as we think we are, we should already know how to love one another, especially if we know how it feels to be loved. If we know how we like to feel about things and know what we like, then we should know how we want and need to be treated—with love and respect—to be happy. A person needs love but does not know how to give it. Shouldn't we give love in the way we would like to receive it?

The movie *The Blind Side,* starring actress Sandra Bullock, is based on the true story of Michael Oher, a young male with a terrible homelife who, after being adopted by a caring and supportive couple, becomes successful on and off the football field. This film shows the benefits of being surrounded by loving people, despite the color of their skin or their sizes. Even if a person acts out of character, there's room for correction, but in love. Jesus said, "Therefore with loving-kindness have I drawn thee" in Jeremiah 31:3 (AV). People are who they are, whether you like it or not; they just are who they are. You must deal with them or leave them alone, and that way no one gets hurt.

When two people meet and they both fall for each other, the moment their eyes meet, both individuals will be able to sense the connection. These mutual vibes will cause both parties to lose their breaths. If you are desperate and in need, the best thing to do is not to meet up with someone, because your feelings are tricky and sometimes treacherous. The feelings that you think you have are only feelings of want, lust, and desire. These are not feelings of need. Lustful thoughts and feelings can cause pain for you and the other person, depending on what's on his or her mind. Slam, bam, thank you, ma'am. One-night stands involve the flesh taking control because you are now in a state of no return, feeling like a volcano, ready to blow its top and explode. You might end up dealing with the consequences of that lustful action for the rest of your life.

If you are lonely, stay lonely, because getting with somebody does not mean that you will be happy. As a matter of a fact, you might just get even lonelier. Some people are married, but they are married living a single life. Just because you have gotten to know someone who you think you would like to spend the rest of your life with, that really does not mean anything if the two of you are not in love with each other. The only thing that does matter is your heart, mind, body, and soul. If your heart is not in the right place, it will explode inside of your chest; in other words, wherever your heart is, there your treasure is also. To paraphrase Luke 12:34, if your heart's on messed-up stuff, expect to have messed-up relationships, because if your heart is not in the right place and your mind is "tore up from the floor up," it is impossible for Christ Jesus to keep your mind in perfect peace, because it is not on Him as it should be.

I understand that I have not yet come to the knowledge of the meaning of the question "**Why me?**" So many times, things happen in a person's life, and the same question pops up—why me? Why are we not examining ourselves to see what caused the problem before casting the blame on someone else? We, as human beings, never, ever want to be blamed for anything. Why is that?

The fact is, a person will always want to be the one who is always right. Though I beg to differ, he who is without sin or has never done anything wrong in life, let him or her throw in the towel or cast the first stone. If you or anyone has cast a stone or blamed anyone other than yourself, take it back; you have also done some wrong in your life. It does not matter what kind of wrong it is. Wrong is wrong, no matter how or which way you look at it. None is bigger than the other; they are all the same size. According to Romans 6:23 (AV), "The wages of sin *is* death; but the gift of God *is* eternal life through Jesus Christ our Lord."

Things always seem to happen in a person's life, and the person probably will never understand it until the Holy Spirit brings it to his or her attention, depending on that person's ability to comprehend or understand who he or she is serving or worshiping. It's God's duty, if you trust in that which you have never seen. God is like the wind; you can't see him, but you can feel the effects of the Holy Spirit. God gives comfort to the comfortless and sight to the blind. I thank the invisible yet visible God. It is because of God's grace and mercy that I serve the Father, God the Son, and God the Holy Ghost. God has never made a mistake and never will, for He is too wise and too powerful to do such a thing. God is an all-knowing god. He is the God of all creations that exist, and He is before anything that has ever existed. He is the alpha and the omega, and before Him, there is no other.

God said in his word that after man had transgressed, He repented because of our wickedness, adultery, and fornication. Our lips move, but they are full of oblivion and are not telling the truth. There is cheating and disregard for a life of equality. We are disrespectful to others as well as ourselves, and we have not kept our word hidden in our hearts. God provides and takes care of His children as He wanted to in the beginning, because He loves and cares for us. Genesis 6:6 (AV) tells us that "it repented the LORD that he made man on the earth, and it grieved him at his heart."

Whenever something causes your heart to grieve, it is usually extreme and painful. If one is not careful, these kinds of things will cause a person to lose his or her very own mind. Everyone has the right and need to grieve. Maybe you tragically lost a loved one, or maybe someone has simply done you wrong for no reason or has called you every name but your own.

After you have done all you can do to satisfy or please your love and have gone out of your way (for example, forgotten about yourself in order to please someone) and this person is still not satisfied or appreciative, then it's time to let time take its place and let bygones be bygones. It is what it is or has turned out to be, and the only thing to do now is to see the big picture and keep it moving, baby!

God has promised us life that we might live it more abundantly. God breathed the breath of life into our bodies and has given us a soul so that we would know how to treat others with feelings of love and morality. We are here for a purpose, and in order for us to please him, we must fulfill that purpose for whatever it might be. God has fulfilled his, which is the breath of life He breathed into our bodies, so we should be thankful for all He has done for us, His children.

In Genesis 1:26 (AV), God said to his son and to his spirit, "Let us make man in our image," which means let's create something beautiful and give it a purpose, a will. Let us make life worth living; let's give them a land that's not made by the hands of man, but by our hands that they might be satisfied with the outcome of it all. God is good, and He will do just what He said He would do to make things better. He said (to paraphrase), "Whatsoever thing you ask in my name, it's yours for the taking (John 14:13), and wherever your feet shall tread upon, it's yours (Deuteronomy 11:24); all you need to do is ask for it and believe, and I will reward it you who diligently seeks me, as well as acknowledges me (Mark 11:24)."

It's not God's will that any should perish; His will is for everyone to have everlasting life. Although many are called, few are chosen. It's not because He has favorites; it's because He does not. If it is anybody's fault; it is yours. God simply wants you to have your mind and thoughts focused upon Him so that He will be able to protect you from your own words. It's your sins that will cause you to be lost, but His love for you will save you. God's word is unchanging. God is the same yesterday, today, and forever, and I cannot and will not go against His word because the truth is the truth.

My Struggles

As I sat and thought about things that had happened in my life, I thought about my childhood, to my first day of school. I was so happy and ready that I had an accident. I wet myself because I was so excited. It was an overwhelming day. I met my first-grade teacher, Mrs. Jackson; she was light-skinned, short, and bowlegged. From what I can remember, she was knockout fine. She was the type of woman any man would have desired to have and to hold till death did them part. She was the Halle Berry of the seventies, so beautiful, and she had a spirit that drew you to her. Oh, how I wish I could have been older in those days!

I can remember being unable to sleep at night, because she was the only thing that was on my mind. She was the answer to my dreams and the mother of my children. I was already in the future and did not know it. I had dreams. Even as a child, the enemy plays with your mind for those who understand. At the age of six, I could not help thinking about her because of how beautiful she was.

In six days, God's creation was finished, and He rested. It was the first day of the last day of beauty, in my eyes. As I thought about how beautiful she was, I also thought about the beauty of the adversary. There's nothing wrong with beauty, but the advantage it sometimes has over people can be disturbing. The Bible says that Satan was seen as lightning "falling from heaven" (Luke 10:18). You see the devil was heaven's beauty. The devil was kicked out of heaven after trying to usurp power from God and because his music was filled with trickery.

I learned that it is not the beauty that really counts, but what it possesses. Is it good or bad? What really matters is that there is not a protective wall covering the heart. The enemy will show you the beauty of the outward appearance, but the inside might be deceitful and not to be trusted. The devil will work you, and as he is doing that, he is trying to figure out your thoughts, but he is not able to read your mind. Yet he tries to make suggestions using the words from your own mouth, speaking your problems out loud while you are in a conversation with yourself. The Bible tells us, wherever your treasure (your mind) is, there your heart will be also (Matthew 6:21). I had found my treasure, and I knew where I wanted my lips to be—right up against hers.

These were my thoughts, even as a child. God desires to use us. So does the adversary, but the adversary does not care about us. It's just that I thought she was an angel of some kind that fell out of heaven. She had curly hair and light-skin, she was slim, and she had a voice that sounded angelic. When she was upset with me, it did not matter. It just kept her closer to me, and as a matter of a fact, it made her even more beautiful to me. I was blinded by her beauty.

Lucifer was heaven's beauty, and because of it, he disobeyed, and he was called the fallen angel. He was kicked out of the kingdom of God because of disobedience. Lucifer's motive had been to take God's throne because of His beauty. Beauty is what traps everybody. It captivates your attention so that you might lust after it. Love is not lust, and lust is not love. Love lasts forever; whereas lust is just the excitement of being able to obtain that which you are after. It makes you feel as though you are all powerful.

I can remember being in the school auditorium. I was supposed to be watching some kind of educational show or movie. Instead, I had a dirty magazine. As I was reading it, I hoped that Mrs. Jackson would see it and sit with me, so we could share it with each other, but she took it from me. This upset me. However, after a while, I was right back in love with her because she was so beautiful, and she was so nice and kind to me. I had never seen anyone so beautiful before, and the beauty she possessed blew me away. I was a little boy who thought he was in love with his first-grade teacher. I did not know what being in love felt like, but if that was what it was supposed to feel like, then, yes, I was in love with her.

As my life went on, I can remember getting out of school and ripping and running to get home to do what I couldn't wait to do— watch *The Flintstones, I Dream of Jeannie, The Andy Griffith Show*, and some of my other favorite shows. I just loved watching television and still do today. It kept me from being bored. It was the closest thing to the reality that I wanted to be a part of. It was because of the lifestyle of shame caused by my family's difficult living arrangement; I couldn't invite friends to my house. My living was not the worst; it was just that everybody else seemed to always have, and I did not. It was sort of like the new Tyler Perry show, *The Haves and Have Nots*. I was a member of the have-nots, and it was not my ideal way of living because I always wanted to live in a better environment. Everybody else had so much more. Though others had a more up-to-date color TVs, we, as a family, only had what we could afford: a black-and-white television. It seemed like everybody else had more than we had, which caused a lot of pain and shame for me, because I thought that we were so unfortunate.

Although we could not afford a color TV in those days, we came up with the idea to buy some red, blue, and green plastic paper, cut it to the size of the TV, and put it on the screen in an attempt to add color in the clothes the people were wearing. I remember saying that something was one color and one of my cousins saying it was another color. I often had to agree with him because he was the oldest, the meanest, and the biggest. My cousin had the final word in the house I grew up in, and whatever he said or wanted was what happened. No one dared to challenge him. There was no one who would try him, except for the one who was as daring as he was—my daddy.

My father did not take anything from anybody. Being in the army shell-shocked Dad. He had remembered things that happened during the war, and his mind was confused because of it. No one ever challenged him, and my cousin knew that my dad, aka "Uncle Son," was the king, but my cousin was the "prince," second to none. If something was wrong and or if somebody was bothering us, we told Peanut, "the Prince." When we'd tell those bothering us that we were going to tell Peanut, they would say, "I don't care," in their deep southern accents. My cousin would go looking for them in the small town of Pelham, Georgia, where anybody could be found. It's so small that if you are passing through it and blink your eyes, you might miss it. You can drive through Pelham in a flash. It's not a city; it's more like a community. Pelham is a place where pretty much everybody came together and got along with each other as if we all were just one big family.

Like in the movie *Poetic Justice*, starring the late rapper Tupac Shakur and mega star Janet Jackson, despite the hard times, we talked and laughed as if nothing ever happened. When my cousin found the people who had been bothering us, they would be shaking in their pants, saying things like, "I didn't do nothing," or "He storing on me," in their southern drawls, saying it slowly. Saying anything other than that would be cursing, which was something parents didn't play, back in that time. When it came to respecting your elders or those who had authority over you, it was a must, and there were no ifs, ands, or buts about it. In my youth, growing up in that community, we learned from our upbringing to treat everybody as if they were somebody and no less than that.

Respect is something everybody should have, because without it, our world is hideously ridiculous. For this simple reason, it shows the type of environment or air you've been breathing, for a person is known by his or her associates and who he or she listens to.

Life is too short, but it is also amazing. The end is closer than you know, and now you're wishing and hoping you could have done things differently or better. If you're in your thirties, forties, or fifties, time has now passed, and you're wishing in one hand and hoping in the other, as my grandmother used to say. Which one is worth more—the wishing hand or the hoping one?

Sometimes life itself might stink, but at least, it's worth living and working for and working out. A marriage or a relationship is not going to smell good all the time, but at least, it's something to work on. For example, Noah was on the ark with all those animals. Do I need to say more? He was in the ark, but what happened when it was time for the bathroom? Did he leave the ark? It is the same with a relationship that is precious and promising. There is no difference.

If you are in a relationship with someone, then you have good standards, and without them, you would have what I would call a "situation." This can become a problem because I have never known a situation to ever be a positive one. It's not the fact that anyone didn't do what he or she had to do; it's just that it's too late now, and you would have to try new things and stay focused on whatever it is that you're doing to stay positive. One way I found out how to stay focused on life was to try and keep my mind on Jesus, knowing that if I have ever fallen short of anything, He would give me peace about the situation. What He has for me is not for anyone else. No devil in hell or on Earth can take it away, because God has got the whole world in His hands.

I had to realize that I am in His hands. John 10:28 (AV) states, "And I give unto them eternal life; and they shall never perish; neither shall any *man* pluck them out of my hands." This lets us know that God really cares for us, His people. Do you belong to Him? Alternatively, which of the two powers do you belong to—the power of the devil or the power of the almighty God? God's power will never end; one needs to ask oneself, when turning to the devil's will, who am I leaning and depending on?

Forbidden Things

A man should not look at a woman's beauty, curves, lips, hair, or her feet with lust in his heart. To look upon a woman is all right; it's the second and third time that makes it a problem, because now it's a desire. For instance, David looked at Bathsheba in 2 Samuel 11:2. One evening after he woke up, he got up from his bed and walked around on the roof of his palace. On the roof, he saw a beautiful woman bathing in her birthday suit. She was appealing to the eye. He sent someone to investigate her, but there was no need, for his servant told David, "She is Bathsheba, the wife of Uriah the Hittite."

David sent messengers to get her. She came to him, and they slept together. However, he did not know that her bathing symbolized purification of herself, meaning she had just finished her monthly menstrual cycle. She became pregnant and bore Solomon. It is forbidden even to look into the eyes of a woman because of the captivating allure that causes weakness that tends to trick and deceive the very essence of man's strength or inner being. This allure encourages and motivates him. A man is designed to do this when it comes to the opposite sex. He is supposed to challenge her. He goes after what's before him and what is pleasing to his eyes, which causes him to think of every word he can in order to get what he wants. This is a challenge to him, and nine times out of ten, he gets what he seeks because a woman loves to be challenged. It pleases her and gives her excitement knowing that he is pursuing her, by any means necessary. Temptation is a desire to have that which is forbidden, so we challenge it to prove what we are capable of, in the same way that the devil challenges God.

Beauty will cause a person to be lifted or to take a fall. It was Mother Eve's beauty that caused Adam to give in to her. It was the beauty and persuasion of Delilah that caused Samson to lose his strength. It's all about what a man sees. Because of his need to dominate and conquer, he doesn't want to lose out on anything. It is a shameful thing to him if he loses.

Women are stimulated by touch, and men are stimulated by sight. A man gives a woman a house, and she will turn it into a home. If a man gives a woman his sperm, nine months later, she will give him a child, and the beat goes on. If you give woman groceries, she will turn them into a meal. What I am trying so hard to say is that women were made to be led by men. One woman for one man, but not the other way around. Men are supposed to be suppliers, and women are supposed to be multipliers; this is the only way that Earth can be replenished.

God's gift to humankind is for us to give pleasure and to make sure that the opposite sex is satisfied. A woman should not be thought of as weak (maybe physically, but not mentally). A woman's way of luring is by the gestures and movement of her body. A woman can see a man looking before he knows she sees him and knows he's looking, which is why she lets him know that she is not where he's looking. For instance, how often have you heard a woman say, "I'm up here, not there," referring to her cleavage? Men are distracted by, yet attracted to what's in front of them and are mostly moved by sight. On the other hand, women are mostly moved by touch, because of the way their minds are equipped. This need to please the opposite sex can also cause a man to be misled and pointed in another direction. His inability to focus on the situation and not friction happens because of his forgetfulness. He forgets his need for mental strength as well as physical strength.

Man can stand his ground physically, but he is not mentally stable or able to take on a woman's persuasions when it comes to her flirtatious ways. In the book of Proverbs, it tells us that the lips of an immoral woman drip honey, and her mouth is smoother than oil, but in the end, she is more bitter than a wormwood and is as sharp as a two-edged sword (5.5). In the beginning of any relationship, it is not good to look upon a woman because of her looks or for her to look upon a man because of his looks or because of his smooth words of deception that are perceived as being cute, charming, and challenging. It is known and recognized that women love challenges. They love being pursued, which is all to test your worthiness. If you are worthy to have her, you are tested, tempted, and tried. If the challenge is not worth it, then you are weak and sending her false signals.

It is only when two hearts can beat as one that we should pursue each other, but due to the wantonness of the two parties, they pursue each other regardless. This brings me to another portion of a kind of a forbidden thing. Do not go after what's not coming after you simply because it will be devastating. There are times in our lives that will be challenging, daring, and complicated. Sometimes we give in to temptation because it seems right, because of its presence at the time, but it does not mean it's good for us. Just because things look good and shine does not mean they are gold or diamonds. Who knows? It could be fire, but because some things in life are so tempting, we fall for it and do whatever it presents to us. And we give in to it, and nobody can tell us otherwise. So we keep walking over the cliff until we fall over, and it's nobody's fault but our own.

Another thing that is forbidden according to the Bible (and I have probably already talked about this) is same-sex couples having a family. It corrupts others as well as the children. Children should not grow up having two parents of the same sex. It is wrong simply because of the structure and body parts of the two. One should be the fertilizer and the other the garden. Every garden needs fertilization in order for anything in it to have a chance at growth.

Let me say that it is forbidden to even drink water that you know is not good for you. You could be in a desert, dying of thirst, but if you knowingly drink "bad water," as time passes, you will pay the price. Isaiah 5:20 warns about calling something what it's not. It simply says in the King James Version: "Woe unto them that call evil good and good evil; that put darkness for light; and light for darkness; that put bitter for sweet; and sweet for bitter!"

After reading Romans 1:25, the following questions can be asked: Who changed the truth and made God a liar? Who worships and serves the creature more than the creator? Who was it? And who changed the truth into what they wanted it to be? Sometimes the small things in life are the easiest to find or figure out because they are the least expected. For instance, just because you are in a chicken coop does not mean you're a chicken. Sometimes we change the truth into what we want it to be, but that still does not make it right or true. It's still what it was before you changed it. No matter how much or how hard you try to change it, it's still the same and cannot be changed into the truth, unless God changes it.

An Infant's Life From My Perspective

The beginning of an infant's life is filled with what's on the inside of his or her mother. It starts from the pregnant mother's conversations with the fetus while in the womb and from the mother's cord feeding nutrients to the fetus. This brings joy and supports its emotions, its soul, and its well-being. The act of her love and kindness is present. It is not good to intrude or to interrupt anything that is already in place or in order. The Bible tells us in 1 Corinthians 14:40 to let all things be done decently and in order. Don't get in the middle of progress or just include yourself so that you might have a part in whatever, whatever it is. If it can wait, then it needs to be saved. Everybody thinks that raising or having a child makes him or her a grown up or as big as his or her parents are, but it doesn't. It only makes you as you are because now you are responsible for your own work, damage, or whatever. You are the only one who has to clean it up.

Proverbs 22:6 tells us to train children in the way that they should go. When they are old, they will not depart from it, which will save their souls from the fires of hell and the ways of the world. If they do depart from it, it will cause embarrassment for parents because it will show that they did not properly train their child.

In the '70s, we respected our parents. It showed proper parenting and teachings that were good for their protection, especially since we were black and living in the South. Being disrespectful was bad publicity for your parents and community elders. While living in the South, "Confederate behavior" referred to always having to prove that you're not an untrained animal with a learning disability.

Bad behavior was not tolerated while I was growing up in the Deep South. It seemed as if others had more authority over our parents than they had over themselves. If you were not well-mannered, you would be chastised, and there was nothing anyone could or would do about it. It was said that you were to only speak when you were spoken to. In other words, shut up when grown folks were talking. Whenever grownups were talking, we were not to interfere as we were to be quiet and not make a sound. This made our parents proud of their accomplishment of raising well-mannered children who were recognized by the community as such. Well-behaved children **were** given a pat on the back for being good boys or good girls. The parents were given positive recognition for keeping us under control and quiet with nothing coming out of our mouths. It was very hard being a child and being expected to be still and do nothing. Not being able to speak my mind and say what was on it was devastating. This was the way my life was growing up in the South during the 1970s.

As a black person who lived in the South, I can tell you that there was not always southern hospitality when it came to my rights in the city of Pelham in the state of Georgia. When you got into any trouble, everybody knew it, and everybody knew your parents. Going to school there was not all that bad, but it was not all that good either. Segregation was a way of life in the sixties, seventies, and the eighties.

The girls went to a separate school from the boys. Can you imagine? A school full of black males with a white principal whose name was Mr. Houston. He used a gym belt for chastisement and then switched it to a wooden board because he felt that it was not getting through to us. Then to make things worse, the board of punishment was advanced when holes were added to it, so now, when it hit you, there would be nothing to slow it down. The holes gave it a little more speed and power.

There was a time I got into some trouble and had to go to the principal's office to get a whooping as punishment. I was hit so hard it felt like my hip was broken. I could not sit down for what seemed like days. I think taking discipline out of the home was wrong. I think it should have been taken out of the school system because no one knows children like their parents know them. I believe that if the parents were left alone and allowed to be parents to their children, it would not be the way it is today, because parents make a difference.

The cycle has started all over again. Those with their so-called power changed the law, and with it, they have successfully taken away the law of the home called parenthood. The law has become the real parent of the home. Since this is the case, what makes them any more or less than a communist? My question is, when will we go back to the biblical standards this land was built upon and let the parent be the parent and the child be the child? When will we let freedom ring once again in the ears of everyone and stop trying to tell everybody how they should parent their children?

There were times not to speak, and there were times to speak. Who is to say? As a child I was being protected by not talking. It was my father's but mostly my grandmother's way of protecting us. Although my father played an active role in my life, it was my grandmother who raised me. If I interrupted her, she would let my father know that I was disrespecting her in front of people and causing disgrace and shame on the family, which was worse than being put in time-out. Children are being put in time-out these days, and right after time-out expires, they continue their poor behavior. My grandmother went by the word of God, which said that if you spare the rod, switch, belt, or whatever you have in your hands, then you spoil the child. That rod, switch, or belt was not going to kill them, but it would save their lives and their souls. It will help them stay on the straight and narrow road.

According to Proverbs 22:15 (AV), "Foolishness *is* bound in the heart of a child; but the rod of discipline shall drive it far from him." I am a strong believer in this. The "rod" kept me out of trouble and out of jail; whereas, being foolish and doing foolish things has been ignored and has been taken away from what the word of God says. We have allowed our children to run and live their own lives, and some of them have taken over and are now running the lives of their parents as well. Children have put fear in the hearts of their parents. The parents are afraid to challenge them, because of the law. Some even go to sleep at night, fearing that their children are going to harm them as they slumber. However, if the presence of the Lord was instilled in the children, the fear of God would make them think twice and know that they should never try to bite the hand that feeds them.

I was brought up to honor my mother and father. In my case, I only had my father and my grandmother, who played the role that my mother should have played because my mother was not there. I don't exactly know what happened between my mother and father, but whatever happened probably was for a good reason. People don't stay together anymore as they used to. Maybe it's because the grass seems greener on the other side to some, yet it is dying faster than it is living. It's simple. If you touch what's not yours or what belongs to another, you are already in the wrong. You have misbehaved and committed a sin against whomever it is you are trying to be with. Because you have gone against God's will, you are now a home wrecker, interrupting another man or woman's life because of your selfish desires because you think that you should have or need to have someone else's spouse or significant other more than the other person does. The audacity of uncaring people!

Why is it that we, as people, take pride in the ability to take another's mate? If you think you can take over another person's life, you are destroying a family, and in most cases, your relationship won't last, so nobody ends up winning. You go around in circles and always end up in the same place you left. You think you've done something so great by stealing the mate of another. What a viperous way of thinking. Foolish behaviors are a snake in the grass. I wish my mom and dad could have stayed together, but with life just being life, it happened. It shouldn't have, but it did.

I did not know where my mom was or if she even still existed on the planet, but then God sent me a way to hear my mother's voice on the telephone. At that time, it only took a dime to talk for as long as you wanted, and I found myself talking to her on the telephone for hours. I was excited to hear her voice. Oh, how beautiful it sounded! I don't remember what we talked about, but I knew that I wanted to meet her. My angel had a plan.

In 1977, I was on my way to see the person on the other side of the phone—my mom. I remember being so happy and so excited as I arrived in the city of Syracuse where she lived. There I was walking down the sidewalk, with a red and white bandana wrapped around my right knee, thinking I was proving something to her, like I was bad or something. It felt good to see her for the first time in my life. I didn't know what she looked like in real life; I'd only seen a black-and-white picture, and I used to look at it all the time.

As I walked down the sidewalk, with my luggage and that red bandana tied around my knee, I thought it would make a big impression on her, because I thought it made me looked cool, but it actually made me look like a total jerk. I lived in the South, and moving north was like going to jail; I had to have my guard up at all times. I had to, at least, look and sound like a New Yorker. It was the same way when I moved to Atlanta. As I was going to see my mom, I saw some people sitting outside, playing cards. Though she hadn't seen me before, my mom knew who I was right off the bat. I knew who she was when I saw her because I recognized her from a picture I'd seen of her when she graduated from college. I was so happy to see my mom. It made me feel complete for a little while. Afterward, I started to realize that there was still an absence in my heart because I'd still spent my childhood without her.

Months down the road, I did something I thought I would never have done, and that was disrespect my mom. I remember my cousin and how he used to tease me about my mom being an alcoholic. When I found out, I lost respect for her. Over the years, my mother gave her life to Christ and stopped drinking and smoking.

A few months after I'd disrespected her; I moved back to Georgia and landed a job there, spreading cloths. I moved back to a city that couldn't afford to pay its own electric bill. What a pity. After a while, I truly regretted the fact that I'd disrespected my mom after I'd searched for her for such a long time, and I still feel bad about it. I truly loved my mom, and I would've done anything in the world within my power for her. I love her so dearly. Even though she was not there for me, I don't blame her for anything, because there are always two sides to a story.

In order to know the truth from a person, you should come together and talk it over so that there's no misunderstanding. What is meant to be will be. The Bible tells us to reason together. In other words, let's hear it from the horse's mouth. Let us figure things out together and make it right. In a relationship, it is not good to believe someone else's words over what your significant other is telling you. It causes mistrust. Everyone has his or her own side of the story. Two different sets of eyes and hearts never lie to each other, simply because the two understand each other and know that it's either true or false. In doing this, it enables you to see things for what they truly are. When two people get together, they learn about each other's body language. They know if the other is telling the truth or not.

While I was back in Pelham and working at my new job, I laid my eyes on a beautiful young lady who I had always wanted to get to know during high school. I called her my "high school sweetheart." We ran away together because her mother did not think I was good enough for her. She said she'd heard rumors about me, but they were not true.

Our relationship was forced to end because of something her mother thought she had heard. We had our final night together. If we have not heard it from the horse's mouth for ourselves, then maybe we should hold our peace and mind our own businesses. This is why many people get into trouble and cause confusion for others. Why would you mess up someone else's life, just because your life is not going in the right direction or because you are not getting the kind of love you have been seeking all of your life?

Why not just be happy? Yours is either coming or going; it depends on you. My girlfriend's mother's opinion of me was based on the color of my skin and the rumors of me being up to no good. She thought I was just after sex, but for me, it was not like that. I never fabricated true love like the one that I had for her. I never ran or chased after anyone. If they didn't want to be with me, oh, well! I love you, but if I have to go through extremes to keep you, then that's just it. I will not be the one that's kissing up to someone who really doesn't want anything to do with me. The way I see it, if you want to be with me, then you will not put me through anything you don't want to be put through. You should treat me the way you would want or like to be treated.

In the book of Galatians, the sixth chapter tells us to bear you one another's burden and so fulfill the law of Christ. It also states that if a man thinks himself to be something when he is nothing, he deceives himself. Let every man prove his own work, and then shall he have rejoicing. Don't question me; question the Bible. It also says to let him or her (because the woman was made of the man) prove his or her own work, and then the man or woman shall have rejoicing in himself or herself alone and not in another, for every man or woman shall bear his or her own burdens. It tells us not to be deceived. God is not mocked; for whatsoever a man sowed, that shall he also reap.

So anyway, shortly after we broke up, the last song we heard together as we sat in the car was "Sexual Healing" by Marvin Gaye. It was not that we needed sex; it was just the fact that we wanted and needed each other for strength, love, and happiness. It was what we had together, what we thought would last forever. It seemed everybody was against us being together, and it was hard breaking up. I don't personally remember how we broke up, but we did.

Then, as life passed, I met the woman who would become the mother of my first child. She was one beautiful, chocolate woman with everything a man could ever ask for, want, or need. It lasted, at least, until my son was about six or seven months old, but it seemed like forever. I remember, one night, going to my son's mother's house to talk to her about our son. It was a rainy night in the month of September. I was hurting, in pain mentally, wanting to be with the love of my life. Because of some funny actions, the same thing had happened with her. Somebody filled her head up with junk, trash, and garbage. Whenever somebody tells you about something they heard but never tells you what it was they heard, it's going to end up not being the truth. It'll just be gossip.

Anything can be fixed, but whenever someone fibs on you, it's the hardest thing ever to try and fix because it was supposed to break you. As long as you know that whatever the devil has meant for you is bad, God will turn it around for your good. People will talk about things that are true and not true, just to have something to talk about, and when they don't have anyone to talk to, they end up talking to themselves. They never told me that whatever it was could be fixed, for whatever reason. It is because of being nosy; it causes frustration and confusion in one's mind.

So being the person that I was, am, and continue to be, I have never kissed up to anyone or showed how much I really care if that person didn't also. It can cause you to become twisted. On my way north, I ended up in Syracuse, New York, some thousand miles away from where I grew up. Sometimes when a person sees that someone is in love with him or her, that person might start to play mind games that may have the person who is in love kissing up to him or her to satisfy only that person's needs and not the needs of the other. Two people who are, indeed, together should be able to satisfy each other and not try to get over on the other. So I went to Syracuse and landed a job working at a bank in the downtown area.

When I met my second son's mother, I got jealous of this guy who happened to be a Caucasian man. After living in the South, in a Confederate state, I did not think that it was right for this white man to be with my "sistah." I did all in my power to take her away from him, and I did. I took the woman he claimed he loved and for whom he would do anything. In my mind, she was not supposed to be his. She was supposed to be mine or another "brotha's." I am not prejudiced. It's just the way things were back then, and I didn't know any better. It was that way in the South, and I grew up in that era.

All I could see was that he was probably the descendant of slave masters that took "sistahs" against their wills and turned them against their men, because they could. I was hurt to see this happening, so I went for it and scored. I got the woman and took over his household devilishly. I conquered what I went after and gained stepdaughters that loved me. On top of it all, I gained a friend in the man whose woman I had taken.

So as life proceeded, she and I had our differences. She bought us a car; I kept the car at my place because she did not have a license to drive. She thought I was trying to take advantage of her. One day, she came to my place and emptied a bag of sugar into the gas tank. When I saw the white crystal, powder-like substance inside the gas cap and sugar spilled on the ground along with an empty sugar bag, I knew that it was her. After a day or so went by, I removed the tank from the car. When I confronted her about this substance being in the car, she laughed and told me something I thought I would never hear from her. She said that since she got the car, I had stopped coming around as often as I used to. She thought that I was trying to use her all of a sudden. Now that I had a car, I was supposedly riding other females in it.

I guess, because she paid for the car but did not have possession of it or of me, I wasn't around enough now. So as life went on, I found myself a church home and started going faithfully to every midweek evening service, every Sunday. I became a faithful member to the church, the pastor, to the people in the church, and most of all, to God.

So time did not stop for little ol' me; it kept on moving, and as I became more deeply involved in the church and God's word, I found myself relating to Adam when he was in the garden of Eden. I found myself without a companion, even after I thought that I had done all I needed to do to quench my heart's thirst for love. I became a youth Sunday school teacher at the church. It tore me up to see what was going on in the streets: brothers killing one another, leaving sisters behind with the big responsibility of raising their children by themselves.

So then I left the children with one simple phrase that they probably still remember today. Whenever we had Sunday school, I would say, "Where is the love?" People don't have a lot of love of today. Whenever a subject pertaining to love came up, the children took it to heart. If I've done all I could do to cause others to do wrong and or have criticized them and expect them to do better, then I have fallen short of what I have said in the past and will be accountable for whatever wrong I have done. I will look back on my teachings to see that I have failed for not living up to the teachings in today's society.

Afterward I became a deacon, which I was very happy to become, because to me it showed my progress. It was the blessing God had bestowed upon me. I was making accomplishments in my life, or at least, I thought .

As a deacon, I became a type of leader in the church. The title of leader made me feel things I had never felt before. Because I had always been told that I wouldn't amount to anything, this accomplishment meant a great deal. I thought, Wow! I'm going somewhere, and I am somebody in life. I was a deacon, but I knew little about the responsibilities that came with the title. The Bible in 1 Timothy 3:8

(AV) says, "Likewise must the deacon be grave, not doubled tongued, not given too much wine, not greed of filthy lucre (money)." It also states that they should possess or have the mystery of the faith, with a pure conscience, and let them also be proved—meaning, let them be worthy to carry such a position. Then let them use the office of a deacon, being found blameless, having one wife. Oh, boy, here we go.

As a wife, there is also a part a woman has to play as long as she has life in her body and desires to stay married to her husband. The lifestyle of being a saved wife is a sacred life unto God and is ordained of Him. According to the Bible and God's standards, it's better to have your own wife and for her to have her own husband, so that there will be no mistakes or "stumblings" in his or her life. Anyway, as the Bible goes on to say, even the wife should be grave and not a slanderer. She should be sober and faithful in all things and to let the deacon be the husband of one wife, ruling their children and their own houses well (1 Timothy 3:9–12). This, to me, means to bring a family up in the admonition with God and with respect and in good behavior. In doing so, they will then, in return, receive respect from others.

Becoming a deacon brought great responsibility. Being the man of the house, I needed to do what I thought was God's will in honoring Him. However, my simple mind looked at it in the wrong way. I looked and I searched and I found myself a girlfriend who became my wife after six or seven months of dating. I started to feel like I was wrong for having a wife, because I was now a deacon digging in forbidden bushes.

I met a little lady who was appealing to my eye. She was about four feet eleven inches tall. I thought she was a winner. I thought that, because she was short, I had to protect her and give her the kind of love she deserved to have from her man. As her husband and the man of the house, what I said was supposed to be what went, no questions asked. Wives should know not to question their husbands unless the husbands ask a question.

My ex-wife was from Brooklyn. I found out later that most women from Brooklyn often seemed to think their stuff doesn't stink. Brooklyn's in the house! Yeah, right! Give me a break. In my experience, a woman who thinks of herself as being bad doesn't really keep a man. Now this is just the way it had me feeling because my nerves got touched, or maybe even the men can't keep the women. Brooklyn women stick with Brooklyn men. I'm not sure if it was some kind of a stick-together-no-matter-what, don't forget your roots, there will always be us, show your respect. At least that was how it seemed. To any others that were not from there, they were misfits, and they would see that the women from my experience had a control problem within themselves. They wanted to be the bosses. I was wrong. Why not be a woman and let a man be a man? How can you try to tell him how to be a man? This became a problem because we didn't know who we were. We were both experiencing identity crises. Not knowing who or what you are is a big problem, isn't it?

I found her, and we dated until one day, when I was getting ready to go home, I gave her a kiss on her forehead. This was my specialty. It helped me see if a woman really wanted to be with me. She talked to her girlfriends about me. She wanted to know if I was gay because of that move I made on her. Her girlfriends told her that she should invite me over to spend the night with her. As time progressed, she talked me into staying the night with her. I said yes, but because I am a man of God, "a leader" in the church, a deacon, I thought I had control over my body. I thought I would be able to resist the temptation, even though, deep down, I knew what was going to happen. She was everything I admired.

On Saturday night, I listened to her and took a bite of the apple, meaning I did something I shouldn't have done. As nature called, I answered it. I went to sleep, thinking that I had it made, at least, until the early morning before the first appearance of daylight. She didn't sleep the whole night. She spent the whole night wondering how she was going to check me out, how she was going to see if I was straight or a gay. She eventually found out that I had a weak place. I want to say to all who think that they have the power to resist the opposite sex, think again. A man and a woman can only be mates, couples, and siblings, but not friends. The mind wonders, and imagination creeps up on you and runs wild. The next thing you know, the two of you will be slapping skin together, and you are no longer friends, because friends don't do that. Because of this, you're wondering what things are like or could be like if you could just test drive it. And it does happen. The enemy has so many tricks you can't even fathom or begin to imagine.

True to what I had become, being a man of God, I found out that I was not strong enough to play with fire. In other words, in testing temptation and my strength, I forgot that the power I had was not any power at all. Resisting may work if you remain far away, but when close, it has its greatest power on you. Early in the morning, she tried me by backing up to me as she kissed me on my body. She started kissing on me, and things happened. She found out that I was all man and that there was nothing in the picture or on me that stated that I was gay.

Three months later, I found out that my girlfriend was pregnant. Because I did not want to bring any shame to the church or myself, I did something that I would regret doing later on in life. We did not want people in the church to ridicule us or say anything bad about us, so I asked her to marry me. I went down on one knee to present myself as a man ready to take care of her, our unborn child, her two month, and two-year-old daughter. It was a package deal, and I had grown to love them as my own, so I took on the responsibilities like a real man. I did not want my child to be a child born out of wedlock. Three or four months later, we got married for the wrong reasons. We got married because I loved her and wanted to take care of her and her children. I wanted to do some of the things for our children that I'd seen my uncles and aunts did for their children, so they could have what I never had: a man and a woman figure in the household. We got married and started our new lives together as one. We started going to church together. We sang in the choir together. She was a very good singer. We were great together.

We raised three beautiful girls, doing well from the time we were married—until Mr. Misunderstanding got in the way. News flash: Thou shall not covet thy neighbor's wife (Exodus 20:17). Things started changing. There were no more hugs, kisses, or "good mornings." We shared our feelings, pain, and downfalls. We stopped feeling the pain for each other and started focusing on our own pain.

When you begin listening to others, it is the beginning of sorrow, hurt, pain, confusion, and deceit. What others think about your lives together can pull you apart. It goes unnoticed, or and it is invisible to the eye of your heart; when you begin to recognize or see what is going on, it is too late. The Bible tells husbands to love their wives as Christ loved the church and gave himself for it (Ephesians 5:25); this is what I thought I was doing.

I provided food for us and made a way for us both to have transportation. When I first met her, she did not know how to drive or cook very well. I learned both of these things from being raised down south in the city of Pelham, Georgia, by my grandma Carrie, who was born on November 28, 1895, lived 103 years and passed away in 1999. She taught me how to cook without actually showing me because I watched her mostly every time she cooked. I was the one in the kitchen asking for the cornbread crumbs and rice cakes followed by the leftovers in the pan after making homemade cake. In fact, my grandmother made everything from scratch—from corn bread and cake, collard greens, green beans, and snap beans to possums and coons surrounded by potatoes and onions, rabbit stew, smothered pork chops, and chicken stew. I learned it by watching her.

I taught my wife how to cook and how to drive. I probably did not teach her in a good way, but it worked. She learned from the sound of my voice, which steered her in the right direction. She didn't want to disappoint me, and even now, she hears my voice when she is about to do something wrong. I am not saying that when teaching someone something, you have to holler or scream at them, but it was what I knew, and it worked for her as it worked for me. I was raised being told what to do in a louder-than-usual voice, rather than in a soft and humble voice. I probably shouldn't have hollered, but it was a successful mission accomplished.

I can only think of one reason why we, as people, should holler, yell, or scream at one another, and that is when someone is lost, hard of hearing, or needs correction. It is a tool used to get immediate attention in an expedited way because it causes a person to really listen to what is being said. This is why my ex-wife knew what to do when she was about to make a mistake. Yet she did not hear my voice correcting her before she made the mistake of getting a divorce. My mistake was that I didn't listen to the voice that screamed at me before we got married. I knew that when we were standing at the altar, I should have run out of the door that presented itself to me. The door seemed to have been moving toward me when I should have been moving toward it. When we were getting married, all of a sudden, something happened to me when the pastor told her to put the ring on my finger. She tried to put it on the wrong finger. I kept thinking, "If it doesn't fit, don't force it," and, "Just relax and let it go." I knew that I should have met the door more than halfway. Whenever opportunity knocks, don't just let it knock; answer it. It might have some interesting news to offer that can either help you or hurt you. If it's an opportunity to hurt you, it's not an opportunity at all, but it's the adversary trying to trick you. You are the only one that can answer it for yourself. Your nose is opened to a fragrance that only you can smell. We all have to learn from our own mistakes, and if we don't learn, then we will always find ourselves right back where we started. Your nose has become opened like peppermint. In other words, nobody can tell you anything when the imagination has taken over the desires of the heart.

You cannot love someone effectively if he or she does not effectively love you in the same way. For instance, if you get married because the two of you have truly found love in each other and share the same affection for one another, it will work, but not until then. If you get married just because your friend got married, it will not work. It will definitely not work if the marriage is based on lies. If you got her pregnant or you tricked him by telling him you're on the pill and know you're not because you just want to get a free meal ticket or welfare, your marriage is destined for failure. This is the wrong way to get things done, and it is very selfish behavior.

Involving someone in your mess who had no clue is simply devilish. Some things are true in a relationship, and some are not, but there should be no secrets involved in a relationship, unless it's going to be a surprise to make the other's heart happy. There should always be a plan in everything that happens. No one should be tricked into something he or she has no clue about or didn't agree to in the beginning.

Whenever a baby is involved in any plan or whenever a baby is going to be involved in a relationship, it takes two people. It takes a man and a woman, not a sperm donor. It is not the way of God. Two people of the same sex corrupt the nature of God and cause problems for the baby. It seems as if everyone has forgotten about the innocent child. We don't think of what's good for others. Our own selfish ways are probably one of the reasons we have such a corrupt world. We do not pay attention to what is going on around us. God made woman for man, not man for woman. He also did not make man for man or woman for woman, because if He did, there would not have been any way the world would be able to replenish itself. He made Eve from Adam, and they multiplied in the land of promise.

Isaiah 1:18 (AV) says, "Come now, and let us reason together, saith the Lord: though your sins be as scarlet, they shall be as white as snow." This means that though you have made a mistake, it shall be forgiven and remembered no more. The words *white as snow* mean it will be as if nothing ever happened and you are scot-free. However, sinning as a practice is not sanctioned by God. He is not a dummy. He is a forgiving God, and He loves you, but we must remember that He said that heaven and Earth will pass, but his word will never pass. It will establish everything it was sent out to do.

Though you live a wormy life, God's call to repentance will clean the two of you, leaving you as white as snow. God can purify you and cause you to be acceptable in His sight. The Bible said for us to come together, but instead of us coming together, we are running away from each other. Life presents itself to be better on the other side after you have met the one you are supposed to be with. The devil is a liar. And the truth is not in him. We will talk about him a little later.

The Bible says—to those of you who don't and probably have never picked up a Bible—to read it. Ask God to give you His wisdom, His knowledge, and His understanding so that you will know that I am telling you the truth. Make sure you research it for yourself. The wise way of doing things is to not just believe what I am telling you. Isaiah 1:19 says that if you are willing and obedient, you shall eat the good of the land. This means you don't have to be in the state you're in, if you pay attention and are obedient to His word, despite what anyone else says. You know for yourself but are open to hear, because we don't know it all. If we did know it all, then we would not be trying to help one another, and you would not be reading this book right at this very moment. Please continue reading; it gets better.

The Bible says, if we refuse and rebel, that we shall "be devoured with the sword: for the mouth of the Lord have spoken it." Peter cut off one of the soldier's ears after Judas betrayed them. Jesus told him that the sword you live by is the sword you shall die by, meaning for us to treat others the way we want to be treated. The way you treat people will make its rounds and fall right back on the one that presented it. It will not be pretty unless you did the right thing and treated them like they are humans instead of animals.

Everybody wants to be treated as if they exist and are a person, and everyone should be treated as such. Satan will use anyone who allows him to come in and to have a seat at the dinner table or a place in his or her bed. It doesn't matter to him, as long as he gets what he wants. He should not be allowed in the most sacred place: your house. It belongs to you and your family, and it is sacred. When God made Adam, he also made Eve to lie down beside him in a sacred place, and there was no one else there to accompany her or him.

The throne and inner court of your home is the bedroom and altar where things are rectified and free from any stain or blemish. It is your sanctuary, a place of praising each other. Second Corinthians 7:4 addresses who has control over their bodies, according to God's standards. The word of God also tells us to not let the sun go down on our wrath. We shouldn't go to bed angry with each other. Ephesians 4:31 tells us, "Let all bitterness, and wrath, and anger, and clamor, and evil speaking, be put away from you, with all malice." Ephesians 4:26 tells us that we can be angry but without sinning. It tells us not to let today turn into tomorrow with you still being angry with each other; if you do, then you have already given praise to the devil that will never be for you but is always against you in everything you do. He will laugh at you as he steals your joy, peace, and happiness.

The enemy never is there for you, but he is always against whatever you do that's good and pleasing to God. Whenever you try to do something good, the enemy is there to prevent it from happening. When you know you should give God praises, he is there to try and stop you. Although the devil is not omnipresent, his imps are widespread. When God created the family, He told them to not let anything or anybody cause you to separate. If one decides that he or she is leaving and has tried his or her very best to keep the family together, there is nothing else that he or she can do. You cannot hold anyone against his or her will; neither can he or she hold you against yours. The Bible tells us, according to 1 Corinthians 7:15 that if you are a believer and if the unbeliever departs, let him or her depart. A brother or sister is not under bondage in such cases, for God has called them to peace.

In John 10:10, the family wrecker presents himself, according to 2 Corinthians 11:14, *declaring that we should not be surprised or marvel, but he is disguised as an angel of light in order to get God's precious treasure. Then he would come looking as if he has everything you (woman or man) need, for the eye is sometimes deceived.* He knows what it takes to steer you away from what is real. Because he makes it look appealing to you, it seems like the right thing to do. It even smells like the right thing to do, and it presents itself to a person's thoughts.

A prime example is Proverbs 23:7 that tell us, "For as he or she thinks in their heart." It says for us to eat and drink, but his heart is not with you. Whatever happens in a relationship and however it happens, we should be mindful of the jealous one who is our adversary and not our advocate, for he is not a friend to anyone. Even before getting yourself into a relationship, pay attention always to what is going on around you at all times, simply because the grass is truly not greener on the other side, but it is unseen in its true identity. What looks good on the outside is not always the way it is on the inside; sometimes, it is the exact opposite.

The Bible tells us that whatever you sow, you also reap, which means, whatever you plant is what will grow. That's if you planted it in good soil. You can't just give or tell everything. It's like giving a fat kid too much cake. Whenever anyone presents himself or herself as the one, believe it, because he or she just might be the one that you probably should not have given a chance. Who knows? These things can also be tricky. Second Corinthians 2:14 says that we shouldn't be surprised because Satan himself has transformed himself into an angel of light and looks promising, but his mind is as rotten as the cores of hell and is only meant for your evil and not your good.

The Bible says, in the book of Genesis, "But as for you, ye thought evil against me; *but* God meant it unto good, to bring to pass, as *it is* this day, to save much people alive" 50:20 (AV). Whenever a person tries to do something to you that is not right, God will turn it around and make it right on your behalf, especially if you serve Him faithfully, because the Bible is not, I believe, for those who have nothing to do with Him because of their own ways and situations.

Psalms 105:15 (AV) reads, "Touch not mine anointed, and do my prophets no harm." It also says in the Synoptic Gospels (Matthew, Mark, and Luke), particularly Matthew 18:6, Mark 9:42, and Luke 17:2, "Whosoever shall offend one of these little ones which believe in me, it were better for him that a millstone was hanged about his neck, and that he were drowned in the depth of the sea." We are His little ones who He cares for and loves. As time goes by, so does life. It just keeps going, even until the end of time or when God calls his little children home for comfort in Him or when He is fed up with the things we just never learn from. There's no doubt in my mind that the pharaoh could have been a better person, but he was just like some of us, stubborn and unable to accept the position chosen for him.

Romans 1:28–31 (AV) says, "And even as they did not like to retain God in *their* knowledge, God gave them over to a reprobate mind, to do those things which are not convenient; Being filled with unrighteousness, fornication, wickedness, covetousness, maliciousness; full of envy, murder, debate, deceit, malignity; whisperers, backbiters, haters of God, despiteful, proud, boasters, inventors of evil things, disobedient to their parents, without understanding, covenant breakers, without natural affection, implacable and unmerciful." As I've moved forward in my life, I've found out that it's not about how beautiful a person is or her height, size, or complexion is. It's about who she is internally. What is important is that two people that are trying to get to know each other should, at least, have a good understanding of one another, even to the point where, if one cries, the other feels the pain and tries to help ease the pain and not let it progress or continue. They should be there for each other simply because it is what's supposed to happen and the way it's supposed to be according to the Bible.

According to Ephesians 5:25–28, husbands should love their wives. My question is, who do you love? Christ loved the church and gave his life for it, that he might sanctify and cleanse it with the washing of water by the word. When one hurts, the other should always be there for his or her partner as if it was his or her own body and not treat the other as if he or she needed to be cut off or thrown away. He might present himself to a glorious church that does not have a spot or wrinkle or any such thing, and as that it should be holy and without blemish spots or wrinkles, so ought men to love their wives as their own bodies.

He who loves his wife loves himself, for no man ever yet hated his own flesh and bones, but he nourishes them and cherishes them even as the Lord the church. For this cause shall a man leave his father and mother and shall be joined unto his wife. They shall be one flesh, and as it is said, what's good for the goose is good, also, for the gander. Marriage is symbolic to the church according to the twenty-second verse of the fifth chapter of Ephesians: "Wives, submit yourselves unto your own husbands, as unto the Lord." Also the Bible tells us to submit ourselves, one to another, in the fear of the Lord. This is the reason why we, as people, should be willing to give a little and wait and not be so ready to receive anything; this is simply because love takes care of itself. You must treat it right, or in other words, you give it the way you would like to receive it. Many times, when we look at what we are doing, we can never see what we are doing. Whatever happened to the original vow?

Bonding

Men Don't Bond, Only Women and Mothers

When two people get married, they come into the agreement that the two of them will love each other as they love themselves. Whatever happened to "until death do us part"? Whatever happened to those promises that were made? Were they the truth, or were they spur of the moment promises, or was it because you did not want to let your friends down or was it because you did not run out of the door when you were supposed to? A lot of things could have been avoided if the two people were truthful enough to really let their real feelings come out to one another.

Now, getting back to one flesh: we should always treat the other as we would like to be treated and not like the other person is just another person fresh from out of the street, living in boxes and eating out of the trash. If we love people who love to be loved, we should know how to love one another the same as we want to be loved, treating one another as if they were us. The Bible said, "Women, love your husbands."

The way I see it is that women, as well as men, should touch each other, for it is God's plan. We mess up when we stop touching each other as we did when we couldn't wait to get each other in the bed. We should never lose that intimacy for one another; because losing that means that the fire is going out. Why should the fire go out unless somebody put it out or somebody saw another fire that seemed to burn brighter or longer? You are no longer a two-minute man but someone else who has built a fire that really has no heat to it, just flames.

The fire and the flame that you have seen and went into is the same one that burns even the same, and the one you accepted is still lit. The fire and the flame are the same and perhaps even brighter and hotter, and the reason they're not the same to you is because you have been blindfolded and cannot see the truth. Romans 1:24 states, "Wherefore God also gave them up to uncleanness through the lusts of their own hearts, to dishonor their own bodies between themselves."

Then who changed the truth of God into a lie and worshiped and served the creature more than the Creator, who is blessed forever? "For this cause, God gave them up unto vile affections: for even their women did change the natural use into that which is against nature: and likewise also the men, leaving the natural use of the woman, burned in their lust toward one another" (Romans 1:26 AV).

Touch Not

The book of **Leviticus** says that you should "not lie with mankind, as with womankind: it *is* abomination, neither shalt thou lie with any beast to defile thyself therewith: neither shall any woman stand before a beast to lie down thereto: it *is* confusion" (**18:22–23**). In other words, when we stop respecting our significant others (our wives and our husbands), the enemy of God has already put thoughts in our minds such as "**I don't need this**," "**I can't do this**," "**You make me sick**," or "**You make me want to vomit**," or any other disgusting, cutting words. It does not help or make it any better. A relationship is supposed to last, and it really should never, ever be about just you. When it is, that is selfishness and self-centeredness.

One way not to be negative toward one another is to try to understand one another before letting the enemy get the best of you. Running away does not solve the problem; it encourages and enhances the problem. It will not be solved until you or the other person accepts the fact that either of you might even be the source of the problem. As long as the problem stays unresolved, it is still there. Wherever you go, it's there because it has not been solved, and it will remain there until it is solved. Some people think they're slick because of their smooth words. As the words make their way to the heart, the ears itch to hear more. It's useful for the time being or, for that purpose and time, fitting to put in your ears, because the words are smooth and will slip right into another's ear as well. After all, they're slippery, and when anything is slippery, it can't keep still. As the old saying goes, "loose lips sink ships." Anything that has no substance has no quality, and anything that has no quality has no quantity. It will amount to nothing–not to a hill of beans or a nickel's worth of dog meat.

Sometimes we get into relationships for all the wrong reasons. Some people get into relationships because of what the other can do for them and not for what they can bring to the table. **Isaiah 1:18–20 tell us that** a relationship should never be about me, me, me, but about us, "twain," two people, and not just one person. It's not about a feeling; it's about being true to yourself and your partner. If it's just about you, it's just not going to work. There's only one person involved with the other one, who is hanging on a string, puppet-like. Pull my string, and I'll do anything. When I move, you move, and without me, you can't move. Don't speak until I pull your string.

Sometimes people think, because of their figures, looks, shapes, or sizes, that that is all they need. Buying things with their looks is difficult to do unless you're advertising. Money can buy pretty much anything that is for sale, but it takes real love to find real love. Pretend love is fake love and can't portray real love. It can look like it and can also feel like it, but real love comes from within your heart, your character, and your inner being. It's when two hearts beat as one. It's called "soul mating" or feeling the desires and needs of another. It's feeling their pains and their emotions and not wanting to hurt each other in any way.

The Bible lets us know that the wolf comes in sheep's clothing; it can look like the real thing, but underneath are deceit, blasphemy, and lies. **Matthew 7:15** calls them ravening wolves. The Bible also tells us to beware of false prophets who will approach as a shining star, so as your imagination, so as he or she will appear, but inwardly they are ravenous wolves. This is simply telling us to look out for those who say that they are someone that they really are not. The story tells us to look out for fakers and haters. Look out for those who pose as roses when they are dandelions. Something that only looks beautiful can really be plotting to kill without warning.

Haters hate to love. They love to hate as well, which is a misconception of the hater's mind. They think that what they want is supposed to be theirs without warnings and as if things are supposed to just come to them because of whom they are or what their names are. Who are you? I am reminded of a story of one that was so beautiful and pleasant to be around. He played music that healed to a point that if the dead heard it, they would rise to the sound. He played the kind of music that would send you on a journey from which you would never want to return. He played instruments that had never been heard before. He could make music that would make a dog talk, a cat walk on its hind legs, a horse gallop, and a bird never fly again. The music was so relaxing. A lot of the times, we would let the pleasant-sounding music captivate us and cause us to lose out on what we had. So we got what we wanted, but we lost what we had. What you had was, indeed, all you needed.

Whenever someone is confused, it's because that person has lost his or her contact with the world and has no pleasure in things that are good for him or her. A hater is someone who has not experienced love or has not been taught love; instead this person has been taught the opposite of what the true meaning of what love really is. A hater is one who does not like to see anyone have anything that the hater does not have. People described here are those that are envious, conniving, and not trustworthy because of their desires to hurt and not love.

A double-minded person is unstable in all his ways. This is discussed in James 1:8. How can you have two brains or two minds? You can't, and that's what makes it so monstrous. A person within a person is scary, because this condition causes a person not to be him or herself. This is why I believe it's not because of the full moon, but it's because of the person allowing the enemy to speak to his or her mind. The full moon did not make you do it or act on anything; you did it.

There was a man who lived in a graveyard who was cutting himself time after time simply because he was so wrapped up in himself. It was as if it was just the natural thing to do for him. Sometimes we can get so wrapped up in ourselves that we forget about the ones who we really love and care about. This can cause a lot of chaos. It's time to come out of the graveyard. In other words, it's time to come out of our selfish ways. Live a life among the living and come out from among them and "be ye separate." We have become the walking dead among the ones that really love us and have cast them away as if they never existed.

The devil's home was once heaven. He knows what it's like there, and because we are the redeemed of the Lord, heaven can now be our home. He know what heaven is about but doesn't want you to have a part of it. Mark 5:5 tells us that there was a man who lived in the mountains and in the tombs, who was always, night and day, crying and cutting himself with stones. Sometimes we, as a people, can cut ourselves when we give in to smooth-talking people, not knowing that those are the ones to watch. Watch them.

The here and after

Years had now passed since the woman of my life had given me everything I had ever asked for. Everything was in place, from top to bottom. I mean, the cups were sitting right. The hind parts were in place. The facial structure was intact. What else could I ask for? Order was in place, but as time passed, everything else fell into the hands of another who had similar promises as the first. It only looked more rewarding, with better promises that were caused by a blind spot caused by greed. Greed will cause anyone to fail. It's greed that makes you feel the need to have and to hold that which was not yours in the beginning anyway. Just because the star is bright, it might not shine. It's just glowing, wondering who sees it; it's a flirting star that has the same characteristics as a chameleon that never can stay the same or tell the truth.

What is it that seemed bigger and brighter? The same star or spark that was seen before was still there. Beware of the wolf that wears sheep's clothing. The first was the order that was not in sheep's clothing but was the clothing with the sheep in it: the real thing that also failed to see the truth. You will not see it if it was staring you right in the face. We only see what we want to see, which can also cause blindness if we keep walking with our eyes closed to what's real and what's not. We will continue walking, and if we are not careful, we will walk off the cliff without any knowledge of it being there, because we refuse to see the truth. It's there, but the enemies have taken over your natural and spiritual sight and assumed control.

The Bible says that we have eyes to see but see not. It tells us also that we have ears to hear, but they work not. **Matthew 11:8** tells that because of their desires for things that seem right to them, God has given them the spirit of slumber, eyes that they should not see, and ears that they should not hear unto this day.

Even as you read this, remember that also the Bible tells us that the eyes have not seen and the ears have not heard, neither has entered in the heart of man, the things that God has prepared for them that love Him. A real man will give his all, even his favorite dish. He will give his last favorite whatever to the one he truly loves, and he will share his life story with her and entrust her with it. Because he cares for her, he will even share the deepest things with her because he loves her and really feels she loves him equally, if not more. R. Kelly wrote, "When a woman loves a man, she loves him for real," and I believe that to be true. I, also, believe that when a man loves a woman, he really loves her, because he gives her his whole heart and not just a portion. This is the real reason a man loses his mind when a woman betrays him and the love he shares with her.

The man is still a man, but this is not so in some cases, **and** he can no longer be considered a real man. Even his own mother has renamed him unknowingly, because she has accepted the fact that he, too, is a dog because of how she has been treated by others. He has been mistreated by a woman who took advantage of his true self at one point. Sometimes we have to be more careful of how we treat people because it will come right back on us unexpectedly. If you don't like being called any name other than the name you were given when you were born, then why call others names? We need to really learn how to treat each other as we would like to be treated. I understand that some of us really don't know how to do that. It just simply depends on how a person was raised; it starts at home. No home training equals no respect, and no respect means a lack of regard for others.

Deceitfulness

The dog chases the cat, which is why now the dog hides, but the cat covers up. When what's been hidden is found, it proves and confirms the hurt. When the covered, which has been buried, is dug up, it stinks worse than the hidden, because the hidden was not covered up, just hidden and able to breathe. Whatever is covered up will become stale, stagnant, and funky, and cause you to gag when it is dug up. It has been given the chance to decay and rot because it hasn't been able to breathe. In a relationship, if things have been buried and hidden for too long, they can start to stink and bring forth impurity.

"I need some time." What does that mean? Women may say, "I have seen someone I like and want to try," or "You are crowding me too much," or "You don't turn me on like you did the first time," "You're not enough of a bad boy for me," or "I want an actor or someone that can, at least, pretend to be someone he is not." The whole thing about a relationship is that a woman doesn't want to feel that she is any less of a person than a man. This is another reason a woman wants to do a man's job or wear the pants in the home. That's all right to a certain extent, as long as she knows her place as a person.

If a woman knows her place as a woman and a man knows his as a man and the children, if there are any, are taught their places in the family, they will have to navigate to reality effectively in order to improve the world. This is true for Americans, Spaniards, Chinese,

Japanese, natives, Africans, or whatever nationality. It will make the world a better place, not only for oneself but for the whole world. The life we live can not only be a better one but also a more exciting one. Prayer will be back in school; discipline will be back in the home. Love will be in the air with the surroundings of peace, joy, and happiness. Sometimes we have to suffer the consequences of things that are going to happen.

Anyway, nothing is going to change unless we come together as real people who want real lives together–two people living lives as one. If you are hurt, I am hurt. If you are crying, so am I. If you are mistreated, so am I. If you are talked about, so am I. You complement me, and when you are seen, so am I. I feel your pain, and you feel mine.

There are no secrets kept from each other because secrets shake foundations, and when foundations are shaken, things are moved. When standing on a sure foundation, it is settled, and it becomes immovable, like a tree, rooted and grounded. We have become, as **Jeremiah 17:8 (AV)** puts it, "as a tree planted by the waters, and that spreads out her roots by the river, and shall not see when heat cometh, but her leaf shall be green; and shall not be careful in the season of drought."

For the Lord said that He is the Lord that searches the heart and tries the reins and gives to every man, according to his ways and according to the fruits of his doings (Jeremiah 17:10). In other words, the things we do as people will be charged. We will be accountable for our actions, and we will face the throne of God for the ultimate conclusion of our actions. We will all face the Almighty, whether we want to or not, because then we have no say so or repentance. When all's said and done, it will be too late to ask for forgiveness, if you have not repented.

I moved forward with my life, ten years later, after a tumultuous experience with a person I thought I knew. Ten years seemed pretty slow, but then I realize it really went by too fast. The pleasure of meeting someone else was constantly on my mind daily. I met who I call the "caviar of my life." I have watched in the tenth year of my life of being alone. I met yet another one that was to be the last one, meaning until death us do part, to the end of our lives/my life or until one of us passed away, because a person should never get married just to say that he or she is married.

I've journeyed through life facing the truth, trying to be the best person anyone could ever ask me to be. I found myself a good job while already working at a job for, at least, twelve years. I found another job, and I have been there for at least ten years. I am now moving forward with my life and going to college to become a substance abuse counselor. After I met the love of my life, who I'd seen and wanted to talk to a number of years ago and finally got a chance to meet her, it was a glorious occasion and a pleasure to meet her. At least, I thought.

We met because we worked at the same place. After becoming close acquaintances, I found pleasure in her eyes when it came to her and me. One day, I had to come in to work, and she had to work; she then found a way to be able to work in the same area that I was working in. She asked me if it was all right if she worked in the same area.

Inwardly, I said, "Oh, hell yeah!" I thought to myself, this could be the glamour of my whole life. As time went on, she stopped asking if she could work in my area and just started coming over. I started wondering, "Oh, my God! Could she really be the woman I prayed for?"

She was the right size, and I am just being real. This is the way men think most of the time. Men would really like to fess up to the truth of how we really feel inside, but we can't because, if we did, our feelings would get tampered and played with by the ones we really cared for and loved. If I was not in the Lord, I would not be saying this with all of my heart.

The Bible tells us to put our trust in no man. The Bible tells us in Psalms 118:8 to trust in the Lord and put not your confidence in man or woman. This even applies to the so-called princes or pretty boys, who think they are all that. When push comes to shove, it's pretty much what is being done, pushing and shoving and no real loving.

The Bible clearly tells us in the book of Romans, "For that which I do I allow not: for that I would, that do I not; but what I hate, that do I" (7:15). This is clearly saying that, even though the things that are being done, I detest it but cannot control, everything that is not God-like will have its day because I gave up the rights or access to my mind to Him who rules and has given me feeling. I cannot refuse, yet I still do it. There are a lot of things we as people do that do not feel right, and we know they are not right, yet we still do them simply because they give us the right to do whatever we desire to do, just to be able to think that we have accomplished something other than what we did as we grew up to be adults. We do those things that displease in order to please, which is blind pleasure. The Bible asked a question and that question was and is, who changed the truth of God into a lie?

There is nothing wrong with being independent, but there is something wrong with going against authority. If we are told not to do this or that, why is it that we do just the opposite of what we were told not to do? It's all about a challenge or because we have arrived, or because we have overcome everything and don't have to listen to anyone because we have reached maturity, or because we have gone through childhood and are so grown now that we don't need to listen to anyone anymore. What is it and why is it that we have become our own gods and now have no one to repent to? Pharaoh had that same problem, and because he had that same problem, he was rejected by God because his heart became hardened and his ears would not hearken to the voice of what was right, which was and is God. A lesson to learn is to always listen before acting or reacting to something that doesn't even feel right, which is a reason not to listen to it because, in your heart, you know it is not right anyway, but because of selfishness, we give it a try because it is a challenge.

The Worship Experience

Who has worshipped and served? The things we did and are doing will cause us to lose out on what God has for us. The Bible tells us that God gave them up unto vile affections. Even the women changed the natural use into that which is against nature (Romans 1:26). Some people have gotten beside themselves, thinking that they are all that and that there is nothing anyone can tell them. Men with men, working that which is unseemly and receiving in themselves that which belongs to women. It is time for us to wake up.

Noah preached in the wilderness for one hundred and twenty years, crying out to the people who had ears but did not get the big picture of what he really was saying, and the same thing is still happening today. He *who hears will listen, and he who listens will hear what is being said to them, but because of so many things going on in our lives, we are too busy to hear what the Lord is truly trying to tell us.*

I continued looking and searching for my true love. My coworker and I started talking and learning and finding out more about each other. Soon after, we started dating. And for the first time in my life, I thought it would be nice to buy some roses. I thought that giving her roses would help kick the relationship off a little better. I wanted to let the roses speak for me.

So I bought her a bouquet of mixed roses—some red, some yellow, some white, and some pink. I wanted them to speak for me. The red meant that I wanted her to be mine, just for me, and the love of life.

I wanted and desired to romance her. She was everything to me and all I ever wanted, because I thought I needed her, but she turned out to be the biggest problem ever. I'll tell you about why she became my problem and not my better half later. Anyway, so then the bouquet was filled with different colors. It was absolutely beautiful, but the meaning of them took me for a spin.

She was beautiful, too, but I did not know her. Well, I'll tell you about it later. As I found out the meaning of the colors, it followed and was to the point: beauty was what I wanted, let alone understandings of the heart. I wanted more than I needed, and it caused trouble in "paradise."

My wants outweighed my needs, and instead of getting or looking for what I needed, I looked more for what I wanted, which was not the real thing. A chameleon, an impostor, appeared in the form of what I was looking for, pretending to be and have everything I had ever wanted and thought I needed. I was more focused on the outer appearance. I placed beauty over substance. It all ended up being an act, an act I was familiar with. It was a game that I myself had played, in the past, in order to have things my way. But it also got me in a bind and a world of trouble because it presented itself to be all that I or any man needed but turned out to be a bag of bones.

The Enemy

The devil is anything that covers up the truth. He will give you a look-alike, just what you didn't need or ask for. As I thought about beauty, I thought about the splendor of it all that turned out to only be a promised look-alike that was just a look-alike and nothing else, not real. She was just a pretender covered in paint. I didn't know it was war paint versus paint on/paint off for beauty. Then she wore nails of aggression, not of suggestion, that needed to be investigated. She had a fake persona that turned out to be unrecognizable and unreal, turned good taste to wasted taste, time that wasted everything that was advertised was only advertised to get attention.

It surely got my attention because it was just like the people who model to get the attention of the bystanders. The models who model clothes that fit them only whereas advertised is real but is a fake and play games that alter the mind, causing the mind to think and wonder, What if? That lingers in the minds of those who are interested in what is seen, but when the paint starts to peel and the beauty is gone and the other side that was covered starts to show and the stench starts to rise from being covered for so long, something never smelt before, then what? Sometimes, we see things happening, but we sometimes fail to take care of the problem. Why do we fail to see the truth? I believe we don't like to see the truth if it appears to be something that will harm ourselves. Sometimes we need to see the truth as if it was ourselves and as if we were in the same predicament. If we, as a people, were in a difficult, unpleasant, or embarrassing situation, we would hurry up and try to fix it because now we are feeling guilty, but why do we have to wait until it gets almost to a point of no return?

The Truth Of The Matter

Sometimes we would rather choose the uncommon rather than that which is common. A prime example can be found in Romans 1:25. It asks us the following questions: Who changed the truth of God into a lie? Who worshipped and served the creature more than the Creator? Who is blessed forever, amen? Why do we continue to reach out for those things that we know we can't have or which are forbidden? Let's say you fall in love with someone who believes in something totally different than what you believe in. This person will cause a world of a change in your life, no matter how much you might think that you are in love, and yes, love hurts sometimes, but not all of the time.

Every word that is said now is a joke or unreal, and it seems like there is nothing you can say that is right, probably is not going to be right. It was ignored in the beginning when you thought you'd seen something, and even though you saw it, you refused to believe what you seen was real. And maybe it's not, and it will change. My answer to that is that it is what it is, and no, your eyes are not playing tricks on you; you're playing tricks on yourself, and you have allowed the mind to take over because it just can't be. But if your eyes are the doorway to your soul, then your eyes are not playing games with you. It's just time to wake up and smell the real world, with all of its games and tricks, being that it's the kingdom of the enemy, who is the accuser of the brethren.

Revelation 12:9–10 tells us, "And the great dragon was cast out, that old serpent, called the Devil, and Satan, which deceives the whole world: he was cast out into the earth, and his angels were cast out with him. And I heard a voice saying in heaven, now is come salvation, and strength, and the kingdom of God, and the power of his Christ: for the accuser of our brethren is cast down, which accused them before our God day and night." These are some of the reasons why we can't have everything we ask for, because they're not good for us, which is why the devil and Satan were cast out. Michael, the archangel, and his angels, according to Revelation 12:7, say that it was because of a misunderstanding that war broke. Michael fought against the dragon, whose name was Lucifer, heaven's beauty, the one who was in the presence of God at all times and filled heaven with his beauty. He was thrown and kicked out of heaven and prevailed not. Neither was there place found any more in heaven for him.

When we are trying out for a relationship, we should not test the waters but try the waters. In other words, we should not just jump into anything without knowing something about that person, place, or thing before praying and listening to our inner person because the inner person does not lie. I jumped into a relationship that looked like it held a whole lot of promise. The woman who became my wife came prepackaged with children. Her beauty and her heart caught my attention. That later led to us hooking up. Things were said, things were done, and things that should have been done and not done were just the opposite.

Getting the woman who was of the ethnicity I had prayed for was finally coming to fruition. She was all I ever wanted and needed; at least I'd thought so. As we'd met at the workplace, she began to ask me if she could work in my workstation. I said sure, that would be nice. I talked a little, and we just started to talk and get more and more comfortable with each other, and I started making plans to try to figure out what I should be doing since I had not dated in over ten years because of a divorce, and I was just really tired of getting misused because of my kindness. I thought it was about time to put the past behind me, so we started dating, and to her surprise, maybe two months later, a bouquet of flowers, which used color to express my feelings, was given to her because of how I'd started to feel. She showed the same desire, but I would learn that her desire was actually very different from mine. I became the prey and not something that was prayed for, but she had become something I had prayed for; at least, I thought she had. So then I bought some red roses, along with yellow and blue roses that meant a lot to me. This was my way of expressing myself to her. I was hoping that, because she seemed like an intelligent person, she would understand that the red roses for me had the tendencies of red crimson. It sticks to you forever, and it will not let go of you even if you let go of it. It also says the same about what I was feeling that was (wow) love in a big way, leading me to do things that would keep her pleased, take care of her, wait on her, rub her feet, massage her when she was hurting, talk to her when she was feeling down. So in my own words, I did everything in my power to help her to be the first and, by far, biggest priority in my life. I was willing to do what I had to do to please her. I was ready to do whatever it took. That's why things didn't last, because one side was pulling, and the other side was pushing. Two wrongs do not make a right, and while it takes two to tangle, it also takes two heads to come together and figure things out.

The Three Roses

The yellow rose represents friendship, joy, and patience. It represents undying love that brings one to believe that he or she is embarking upon an unbreakable love, a love that lasts forever, a love that allows dreams to come true. This is a love that's untouched, that sees no hate, no pain, no regret; instead it's a love that does the exact opposite. It's a love that is only touched by the ones who possess it and cherish it, care for it, and do not regret it. The yellow rose represents a love that helps the hurt and does not create the pain. It's a love that is love indeed and truly is for the one it was pledged to and no other. It is seen and felt; it is not blind. This is a love that is heard, a love that is listened to, a love that is jealous, but not painful, although it will be painful at some point and time in life when it is not understood. Love will sometimes hurt, but only for correction, not deception; it's called true "Benadryl love" love that takes the itch and the pain, perhaps swelling away from crying eyes. Charity is sometimes long-suffering, but it is kind, though it envies not itself, meaning it is not stuck up and does not just care for itself but for others as well.

It does not flaunt itself, and it is not puffed up. Love does not behave unseemly, and it does not seek its own meaning. It's not just all about self but about loving and caring for one another, and most of all, love is not so easily provoked to anger, especially when it is confronted with either the anger of the significant other or any others who are interfering with it, and it does not listen to an interferer. Also, love rejoices in the truth and not heresy, for love bears all things for better or for worse. It hopes for the best of all things and not the worst. Love is everlasting, and it never fails, anything else in life will fail, but love will never fail. Love will be with you forever. God said in his words that He would be with you even until the end of time. The Bible tells us that God is love, so if God is love and if we love one another, then it will never fail; it never fails; it is the frailty of the human that fails, and sees things, hears things, and listens to things other than what he or she is supposed to listen to.

Eve listened to a snake rather than to her husband and God, and even though God put the man in charge and instructions were given, they were not kept. If they were twain before and have tied the knot, they are no longer twain but have become as one. They should know what the other would go for and what they would not as per the same. If you have said "I do," then "I do" continues and never stops because of anything simply, because the fire that was lit by a particular match can only be lit by that same match because it was the one that initially started the fire in the first place. Anything other than that is not real or only a look-alike, and it is not better, only different; it's only a "let me see if I have the power to devour."

Blue roses represent a mystery that attains the impossibilities, which is love at first sight. There are no true blue roses, meaning, genetically blue roses does not exist because it lacks the pigment that produces blue color, blue roses does not occur in nature but there can be true commitment if everyone love him or herself and knows how he or she would like to be loved. Then he or she would know how to treat others. Is it the same? Yes, it is the same when a person loves, and this is in my own opinion. When you hurt, your better half should also feel the hurt if you are soul mates and really are trying to make things work for the better, so I hurt. If you cry, I cry; I cry because I don't want you to cry. It's more than an emotional thing; it's me wanting her to feel better.

When you feel down, I also feel down. Whenever you are feeling down and out, and if I am not, then something's wrong. "Examine yourself." If you are talked about, I am also talked about. It's simple if you are talked about. You represent me and I you; therefore, I am talked about as well. It's called being a soul mate.

After seven months have passed by, there's a possible wedding. That came in due time, as life waits for no one, a marriage that could have waited a little while longer, but because certain things happened, things changed, and now you are doing things together, things that started to grow little by little, things that are now commencing and things that are coming together. Now comes the comforting of one to another. If there are children involved, things are worked out together.

We celebrated life together as couples do and as being committed to each other. What's done behind the closed doors of a man and his wife is undefiled, which means everything that could be done, whatever it was, was not a problem in God's eyes because you are married, because marriage is sacred in God's eyes, and whatever is not is sacred, so to say, in the devil's eyes, which is not godly. The devil will do anything in his power to try and overpower what God has for His people, and it would not be a problem for him to take away. You see, he is just the opposite of what God is. God multiplies, but the devil subtracts.

As time grows older and passes, the enemy will make it seem as if things are being done over and over again. It starts to make a person want to start trying and searching for new things, even with a new person who seems right at the time but is not, so things start to grow apart. You start hearing too much negativity and start saying and talking too much, and then suddenly stop doing things together, which is the first trick of the enemy, even at the wedding, believe it or not.

Then there came the whisperers and togetherness, I knew not of. We moved into a place that we should not have because it cost too much to pay out monthly. But she wanted it, and because she wanted it, we got it in order to bring pleasure to her. I did whatever it took; even if it made me miserable, knowing we couldn't afford it. Long story short, we lost our income tax because the head of the household was filed, money was collected, and things were bought. We were satisfied, but then when I filed, and because head of the household had already been filed, we had to pay back, and in our paying back, the other side started to show, the unseen side. The side never seen before showed up. The smell started to grow, the beauty started to fade, the language changed from sweetness to bitterness, and the heart started to pump more than just blood. So now there was no beauty to be found anywhere; the beauty was cast out. Everything that was left tried to take over, rule, and control.

Disrespect validates the unknown things that happen every now and then; things heard were no longer heard, and things seen were no longer seen, which brings up a question, "Was there any love?" And if there was, what happened to it? Change came because of things that were whispered into the ear of a willing listener, and the things that people whisper are things said that should not be heard. Anything that's whispered is a secret, and secrets are not of God simply because whispering into someone's ear causes confusion. The Bible tells us to beware of dogs and whisperers. It also tells us in the book of Philippians in the third chapter second verse, "Beware of dogs, beware of evil workers, and beware of the concision." In other words, watch out for those that will take your good, mutilate it, and change it to be what they want it to be, and once the damage is done, it's just like your worst enemy, smiling in your face and talking behind your back.

Red Roses: The red rose portrays beauty. What is beauty? Beauty can be either outer or inner appearance, whereas the outer is just something beautiful to look upon only in most cases. It gives intense pleasure and or deep satisfaction to the mind. Also it's just an appearance; whereas inner beauty is and includes kindness, empathy, sympathy, compassion, true love, passion, courage, and true respect. It says, "Congratulations. I love you despite all of the circumstances. I love and desire to have and to hold." In Christianity, it is symbolized as the suffering of Jesus on the cross during his crucifixion. That shows how much he loves. He came to die, giving his own life for ours. Love is love. The Bible tells us that God is love. First John 4:16 (AV) states in the second clause that "God is love; and he that reside in love stays in God, and God in him." Red is the color of blood as we know it, although it is not really red until it hits the air, which is the reason it turns and changes, which is just like love. Whenever it loses its power, things change; love becomes stale, incomplete, and powerless, and has no more interest to continue its promises.

When a thing turns to hatred, forgiveness can't be trusted, and it is foul. Whenever there's a power loss in anything, life is lost, and it cannot be recharged, unless there is a sincerity of forgiveness. Without a sense of realness, it will never happen because there is life, love, forgiveness, and the sharing of love. There is love, time after time, forever and forever, and it is a never-ending story; it is no longer a fantasy, yet it is, but only with the one you truly love.

There are times in life when things seem to be better or maybe even perhaps look better than anything in any other's eyes but are not, and are just in your mind and only last for a limited and not unlimited amount of time, and as long as you keep the same love for one another as before, the fire will never go out. This is simply because, if you know what you have, you can never lose what you found.

Whisperers

Beware of those that whisper because the word of God tells us in Psalm 41:7 (AV) that "all that hate me whisper together against me: against me do they devise my hurt." Proverbs 16:28 says that a whisper can separate even the closest of friends. It will separate you even from your best friends forever because it actually tells them that you are a person who sows strife. So then, when all of this is going on, are you then running into not only haters of God, but finding that even your best friends have now become your worst enemies? A friend does not go behind your back and say things to others about you; instead they say it to your face.

The word of God tells us that to befriend the world is to become enmity to Him, and you are not a friend of His but an enemy. James 4:4 (AV) tells us about and calls us adulterers and adulteresses, and asks "know ye not that the friendship of the world is enmity with God?"

Whosoever, therefore, will be friend of the world is the enemy of God. Deuteronomy 5:9 (AV) states, "for I the LORD thy God *am* a jealous God." What I am trying to get the reader of this book to see is that whenever you are about to get involved in a relationship, you should try to learn something about each other. You should seriously think before getting into a relationship because people will get involved with you most of the time, I would say, because of loneliness and not because of love. There is a difference in loneliness and feeling real love, it's another way of getting trapped into something you really don't want or need.

A lot of the times, because we feel something that feels like love, we will tend to believe that it is love, and there is nothing wrong with that except you know for yourself what real love is and what it is not. Simply put, not knowing that has gotten a lot of people in trouble. Samson became lonely, and it caused him, his eyes, his strength, and his integrity to be lost. In doing what he did, which was playing games because of his self-pride, his life was jeopardized because he decided to play with fire.

Games

Whenever we play games, whether they are trying to trick others or trying to make others jealous, we end up losing, knowing that evil never wins anything, no matter how hard it tries. Whenever anyone tries to rush or is always in a hurry to get somewhere or to do something for someone, then it will pay to look at his or her life history. It never hurts to ask questions because it will determine one's future.

In the way I think, there are simple things that we, who really want to be in serious relationships, can do to get to know each other no matter what, because your life depends on it and so does your future with the fact that children might play an important part in it. And the Bible tells us to train up a child in the way that he or she should go, so that when they are grown-ups, they will not have very much to worry about. When two people have come together and surely have fallen in love with each other, they should be able to raise their children without doing anything else that would cause embarrassment or disgrace simply because it was never meant for anyone to step in and take the job of another man or woman, unless they have passed on to the next life, which is why things don't really work out in the manner it was intended to be, and how can you know even if it seems to be good? And if it is good, then imagine how much better it could or would be if everything was in the place as it was intended to be.

I understand that no one person is perfect, true that, but we can still strive for perfection, whereas others, just because things are not going their way, think that it's not right. We have become onlookers to those who are outside looking in on another's life. Then, if they try to change their lives or get jealous of others' lives and if we know them and have not been too much of a friend but an enemy, they will try and cause mischief in others' lives simply because theirs is not right. So when we know what we want, then we can find real love, joy, and peace not only with God but also with our families, the people around us.

Those who you believe have not thought anything about you will have to come forth, because the Bible tells us that He will make our enemies our footstools and He will heat up coals on the head of our enemies and cause them to behave and drop their weapons and flee. God declares He has never seen the righteous forsaken nor his or her children begging for bread or anything. He even claimed us by telling us that He is our God and we are His children, and the last but not least, He lets us know that He will be with us even until the end.

Reality Check

Regardless of what anyone thinks (you, your moms, dads, cousins, aunts, or uncles think), it all comes down to whoever is involved in a relationship. It is clearly recommended that, as a couple, there should not be anyone or anything allowed to come between what's already good. What you see is what you get in a relationship. Despite what anyone else thinks, a relationship should always depend on what the people in the relationship think and not what someone else thinks, because he or she is not a part of that relationship and does not have to deal with the other party of that relationship after it is all over and said and done.

Whenever a relationship is in view or is about to begin, the two should already know one another, and yes, we know that opposite attracts, but what we don't know is that souls connect, too, which is how soul mates are formed because they connect; they know each other, but they are seldom ignored because of the fear of communication and the hurt that happened before, and the only reason hurt happened before is because the heart was not listened to but was ignored. Instead of helping, it caused hurt and distrust, and that caused the mind to start building a wall. It even offered phrases, such as, "You're no good," "I hate you," "All men are the same," "They are nothing but dogs," "Don't have no backbone," "Walls being built," and "It is with the man."

This seems to be saying that all women are the same (playing games, flirtatious, and love challengers).

Now for the man with the woman and her flirtatious ways, know that it would be hard for the man to just say no, even if she already knew that the man was currently in a relationship, because she felt that he should have been hers, which is the same with men, and these are called family and home wreckers who will flirt with you, knowing that you are already in a relationship, trying to see how much power they have, trying out their so-called smoothness. Psalm 55:21 (AV) says "the *words* of his mouth were smoother than butter, but war was in his heart." It also says that "his words were softer than oil, yet *were* they drawn swords." This means the words are being said just to try you and to see if you will give in. Afterward, you will be let down and treated as if you never existed. You have become a puppet, just hanging on a string, but because you have been blinded by what you thought was a light, you have become the prey, caught successfully. You have become the one the cheater has singled out and not because of your flirtatious ways.

It was because you were the most vulnerable, the one who stood out the most in the crowd, the one who showed the most gain, who has proven to be the one, who also ended up as a one-night stand, only for pleasure when needed other than that, just a weekend thing that ended up just another one on the plate waiting to be served and not waited on with pleasure, just an appetizer who knew no better than to just please and not be pleased, just another opportunity. Sometimes in life, we as a people should not have to go through or have to experience things in life only if we listen to our hearts, so how do we listen to our hearts? Well, some say, if it skips a beat, it's a clear indication that the other one did also, because it is of the same, and talking about having the same hearts. Let's look at Mary!

The mother of Jesus went to see Elizabeth, the aunt of Jesus, who at the time was pregnant with a child named John who was the forerunner of Jesus. He leaped in the womb of Elizabeth because of the presence of Jesus in the womb. They had the same heart, seeking to do God's will even in the womb, and that is how it should be when a man and a woman meet. There should be some kind of joy, happiness, peace, or something there that spells out the word connection, love, and commitment.

Something that has something to do with something and somebody such as what is being sought after, and it should connect. "Every wise woman builds her house: but the foolish plucks it down with her hands" (Proverbs 14:1 AV). The Bible tells us in the book of Proverbs 25:24 (AV) "It is better to dwell on the corner of the housetop, than with a brawling woman and in a wide house." And I had to find that out the hard way twice, and because I did not listen to my heart, my nose had been opened.

I just simply went by what I felt. When getting into a relationship, examine yourself, the other person, and the company she or he keeps, and you can never go wrong, but you've got to trust God and take your time, especially if the other one is ready and you are not. It's a sign, and I had to learn it the hard way. So whenever you feel like you are being rushed into something, just simply back away, because you are then protecting yourself and the other. Think with your heart and not your feelings. Be blessed and take it slow.

There are times when, because of our feelings, we really need to break away from everything. Whenever you start to think that you are in this world by yourself or alone, you need to open up your eyes a little wider. The Earth is very large, and it can take care of itself, and sometimes we get the Earth mixed up with the world when it comes to claiming it. Sometimes we tell a person that he or she is invading our world, and sometimes we might be invading his or her world. When your world has shrunk and you feel you can't move around in it, then you have allowed yourself to be captivated in your own little world and have developed what would be called claustrophobia. It cannot contain you. This is called being trapped, confused, and frustrated. Although there are times we/you might feel trapped, confused, and frustrated, as long as you know that there is a God somewhere in your life, there has got to be healings somewhere.

Anything that's not like God is not of God, no matter how it is put. Satan was heaven's beauty, who was in the presence of God at all times, who also made beautiful music, let's say, so that it would be with him at all times. Anytime you think that there is nothing in the world that can beautify you and cause you to feel at peace, then you have given all of your peace away to the adversary. God said that, if you call on His name, He will hear you. Most of the time, we are calling on the wrong thing to help us in life, just as it was your God and you put it before God and that thing you called on or depended on was a false god and idol that the false prophets called on that did not answer their calls.

Whenever you call on anything other than the capital *G* God, it is not real. I believe God to be a real god, like I believe that the wind blows, and because of the effects of the wind, it proves that the wind is there. God, however, does not have to prove anything to anybody. He is watching and listening all the time for He is the Alpha and the Omega that needs no sleep nor does He slumber. He is the God that breathes. He is the one and only God because He has given us the breath of life.

The Bible tells us that greater is the faith of those who have believed and have not seen, than those who have seen and have not believed (John 20:29). The Bible tells us that "faith is the substance of things hoped for, the evidence of things not seen" (Hebrews 11:1 AV). "Greater love hath no man than this, that a man lay his life down for his friends" (John 15:13 AV). My thought is, where is the love? Moreover, what happened to true and real love? Does it exist anymore? And, if so, then I believe God will spare the city and set the captives free.

There are too many times in our little bitty lives that we take love, life, happiness, peace, and hope for granted and end up doing some things we ought not to be doing because we end up hurting people, regardless of how they feel. We do not care anymore about people, or even our own families. Why is it that we can't genuinely love, despite what a person looks like, despite the way a person talks, because it is not his or her fault that he or she talks the way that person does; it was God who gave him or her that voice. When we love, it should be without dissimilation; it should be straight from the heart, because we all have a part in life. If we did not have any parts in life, then why are there women to have babies and men to fertilize them?

A woman likes to get smart and say that she does not need a man to make a baby, and that, too, is a lie because it takes a man's sperm to activate that egg. You see, it is like planting a garden. The seed has to be in the ground, and after that, the seed is planted. Life comes forth, but it has to come from the man because a woman cannot make a baby by herself, and that is final.

God's Wrath

The wrath of God is revealed from heaven to all people versus things that are ungodly and unrighteous, and to those who are not living according to His standard way of living, which is in a holy way, according to His word, which is in the book of Romans, 1:18.

First Peter 1:16 tells us to "be ye holy; for I am holy." As Christ lived, so shall we live, meaning God will pour His wrath out on that which is not like Him for He is a holy God.

Second Thessalonians 2:10 also tells us that God will pour out His wrath on all those who deceive and are unrighteous and that they will perish because they refused to receive the love and truthfulness of God—they refused to be saved.

Also because of the ignorance of humanity, the Lord is displeased in a sense that it made him wink according to Acts 17:30, meaning that man was not acknowledging His word as he should have been. Man flourished and was foolish, according to God's word, and as it was in the days of Noah and in the days of Moses, the people started marrying and given in marriage, marrying just to be able to say "I'm married now" and not marrying according to what the Bible has to say about marrying. You should be hearing the words "Don't do it, Celie. Don't do it," quoted from *The Color Purple*.

People these days and in those days were marrying for the wrong reasons and could not hear the voice of God. Matthew 24:38 states that they were doing this even as the warnings went out, but they paid no attention to the warnings. Whenever people lose track of what's going on around them, it becomes very hard to stay focused on anything, even they, because they have lost track of time and their surroundings and the ones who really love them.

After doing what you or they wanted you to do and not paying attention to what's right and just doing your own thing, God will reveal His promise to pour out His wrath on the land because of the things that are not done the right way, according to His will, as a parent will discipline his or her child if he or she is disobedient. For it is better to be obedient than to be as you see fit or justified according to you, yourself, and I.

Proverbs 13:24 (AV) states that "he who withholds his rod hates his son, but he who loves him disciplines him diligently." In other words, help your son or daughter to come to the knowledge of the truth. The truth is something we as people love and are willing to be a part of. As long as everything is going right and according to our standards, it's all right, but what happens when it doesn't?

"For God so loved the world that he gave His only begotten Son, that whosoever believeth in him should not perish but have everlasting life. God did not send the Son into the world to judge the world, but that the world might be saved through Him" (John 3:16–17 AV). This is saying He loved the world so much that He gave His best, meaning His only son Jesus Christ, who many still do not believe in. He came to this world and saved all the wretched souls, which includes me and you. Romans 7:24 (AV) says, "O wretched man that I am! Who shall deliver me from the body of this death?"

In the book of Romans 6:23 (AV), it tells us that "the wages of sin *is* Death; but the gift of God *is* eternal life through Jesus Christ our Lord." No matter what you say, I want the gift of God, so that when I pass from this life to the next, I will wake up at the feet of the one that came and died for a wretch like me and hear those words, those words everybody should want to hear: "Enter, welcome, you have been faithful over the few things that were put before you, and I made you a ruler over many things inter into the joy of the lord that your labor would not be in vain, and we have reasoned together, and it was all good, so come here ye now and sup with me as I have with you, and let's rejoice together. Therefore, my dear brothers and sisters, stand firm. Let nothing move you. Always give yourselves fully to the work of the Lord, because you know that your labor in the Lord is not in vain. (1 Corinthians 15:58).

So Jesus came into the world to save that which was lost, for the world through Him could be saved. Sometimes we can be out of touch with the spirituality of God. Sometimes we don't realize how close to death we've come or how death has passed us by because God said, "No, not yet. I will give them one more time to get it right with me because I am all."

God is a God of more than a second chance, and He knows that you don't count it as being gracious or giving or think that it's not right because of the things that have been allowed to happen, though it was not meant to hurt you, but to prepare you for what's ahead and the plot that's coming your way, that's far more worse, and He knows that's it's hard but remember that He said that He would not allow anything to come to you that was worse than what you can handle, and He knows that you don't realize or recognize who God really is; instead jokes and other things have been said like "what do I have I to be saved?" It's called stupidity not to accept Him. According to the book of Genesis 6:6, God is angry at man because of what occurred in the land after his creation. In the process of creating, something has to be beautiful, because if it wasn't, then why did God create us? When God breathed the breath of life into us, it was beautiful, and it was even more beautiful because it was the perfection of His appreciation until man did not want to do it His way anymore.

The Bible says that it repented the Lord that He had made man on the earth, and it grieved Him at his heart because of the wickedness in the land and because of the way life was interpreted by man. Also in Isaiah 63:10, it states that the people started to rebel against God and vexed His Holy Spirit, and in return God turned and became their enemy, for to be a friend of the world is to be enmity against God. According to Romans 8:7–9 (AV), "The carnal minded is enmity against God: for he is not subject to the law of God, neither indeed can be." They who are in the flesh cannot please God; there no condemnation of them which are in Christ Jesus, who walk not after the flesh, but after the spirit of God. We are without excuse in serving Him, being that the word of God is before us daily. If the word is before us daily, why is it that we do not see it? What is love if you can't give it? What is thirsty if you cannot quench it? In addition, what is giving if you only know how to receive? The beat goes on.

God said, "Lo, I come: in the volume of a book *it is* written of me" (Psalm 40:7 AV). The word of God is plain to him that understands it according to the will of God. It is right to find knowledge, but first of all, a person who's trying to go forth in life should always reach for the top, and in our reaching, we should probably try waving our hands and out of nowhere tell the Lord thank you and in so doing that we should know that we have to, above all things, get some wisdom, knowledge, and understanding. These are the principal things to get, but in all our getting, the Bible tells us to get an understanding. A person cannot understand anything by not reading or, at least, trying to study the Bible. It tells us to study, to show ourselves approved to God. A workman needs not to be ashamed, rightly dividing the word of truth. I have never seen anyone who can divide an even number into an odd number and get an even number for the answer. This is just like the devil. He will give you something you will never be able to figure out simply because he does not play fair in anything he does in life or anyone else's life because he is not even true to himself, let alone you.

God was and is who He says He is. The people glorified Him not, and they became vain in their imaginations, for their hearts became darkened, for whenever good is present, then the presence of evil is also present. Question is, whose presence are you in? And whose presences are they in when face to face with you and are you yourself, who are you presenting yourself or your supporter in whom awakes you daily (Romans 7:21). Paul said that, "I find then the law, that when I would do good, evil is present with me," so then the people's response to the call of God to repentance was null and void, for they were in a state of rebellion, and for that cause, Matthew 22:14 tells us that many are called, but few are chosen.

As human beings, why is it that we just have to be chosen, and why is it that, if we are not chosen, we get all discombobulated and confused with everything we come in contact with? So then God's verdict is that, because His people are in a state of rebellion, He will give to them according to His word and pour out His wrath on those that refused to do His will and hearken to His voice. Those who have walked with Him, talked with Him, and have tasted, yet have refused to do His will, will suffer the consequences and will pay in the end; it is better to taste and be thankful than to taste it and waste it as if He was never good to you. The Bible tells us to taste and see that the Lord is good. He is good. There are too many times that we just sit around and waste time. Other times we have lost track of time and have gotten lost in a time zone or become trapped in our own little worlds.

Psalm 34:8 (AV) tells us to "taste and see that the LORD is good: blessed *is* the man *that* trust in him." And this is the outcome of His verdict, it is good and just, the opposite if he or she is not so good. God is like this, to my knowledge. If you ask me for something and when it's time for me to give it to you and you refuse it, then why did you ask in the first place? It would have been better that you had not asked than to ask because it is a mind-boggling thing that interrupts the thought patterns of others.

God reveals himself in man when man begins being a witness to Him and His power to heal, set free, and deliver them from depression and that He only can clean their conscience of whatever they are going through and being able to bring them out of their situations. Also, He reveals Himself by way of their beliefs and testimonies of man. Only He can bring them out of a situation that seems impossible because He can do the impossible for man to understand, but because God is who He is; He can do whatever He pleases.

If a person is in a situation and can't see any other way out, all that needs to be done is to call on His name. What's His name? His name is Jesus. Wait for His answer, and in our waiting, we have to know that He has three answers to our question and those are *yes*, *no*, and *wait*, which means *not yet*, and we have to remember that we cannot rush God. Also, we have to be careful of what we ask for anyway, because in all of our asking, God will give it to you if it is for you. What Father would give his children something that would hurt them and not help them? God is a good god, and He is worthy to be praised. Yes, He is. Now give Him some praise. Clap your hands. Try Him.

According to Matthew 19:26 (AV), which clearly states that, "Jesus beheld them, and said unto them, 'With men this is impossible, but with God all things *are* possible,'" it is also revealed that, if you don't believe that Jesus is the Son of God, you make him a liar. The Bible also lets us know that, according to John 8:44 (AV), "Ye are of *your* father the devil, and the lusts of your father ye will do. He was a murderer from the beginning, and abode not in the truth, because there is no truth in him. When he speaks a lie, he speaks of his own: for he is a liar, and the father of it." He lies, and he is consistent.

John 1:18 states that no man has seen God, for He is the invisible God yet visible to all for His mighty act. He is seen in the book of Romans 1:20, which simply puts it as this: He revealed Himself in His son Jesus Christ, who is the brightness of His glory and was more than just an angel, being one that purges sin, forgives sin, and is the doorway to God's promise. He is the bright and morning star, was a being in the beginning with God, and was God in the flesh. He was and still is the rose of Sharon, and He is the lily of and in the valley. Song of Solomon 2:1 (AV) puts it like this: "I am the rose of Sharon, and the lily of the valleys." So what is He to me, me, and me? So then the significance of the two is the same. Choosing God is to choose His son; not choosing His son is not to choose Him, for the two are one or are considered as one because they all have their own parts in the sway of the matter, although they said in the beginning to let us make man in our own image. I don't see how is it that there are even people that will tell you that they are "one-percenters" and there are those that will tell you they are "Jesus-only" believers. It defeats the purpose, and it is really saying that there is no Holy Ghost or Holy Spirit if you want to just make it just not sound so holy, but anyway it's the Father, the Son, and the Holy Ghost in whose names we have to know that exist and have forever existed even before time. "In the beginning was the Word, the word was with God, and the word was God (John 1:1 AV).

John 10:38 tells us that the Father is in him, he is in the Father, and the two are one. Whenever you are in a relationship, you are no longer considered as yourself, meaning you are one. Your identity changes, and now you are no longer twain but are one until death you do part, and that's not by being a taker of life but rather a giver, because you love each other, and it was because of your vows, the ones you made and promised each other. Yes, those vows. You no longer represent yourself but each other because of the bond you committed to each other and the commitment to be loyal. As far as being the one, when you are in pain, I am also. When you feel you just can't go on, I'll be there to help you through whatever it is you are going through, but only if you'll let me. I will be your bearer whenever you need strength. I will be your arms to lift when you are weak. I will be there to rub you in some hot relaxing oils.

When you are feeling tension, I will be there to love you when you need to feel love or just to be made love to, for I am your husband or I am whatever you want me to be for the bed is not defiled, for you are my significant other of the right kind, for God made the woman for the man and not the woman for the woman or the man for the man. For how else can you multiply with the same sex, except you adopt, and even that's not even in my will, for I made the father to be the father of his own child and the mother of her own child that was created by the two of you? Now make me a liar. It was never intended to be as such, but since that's the way you want it, to adopt a child, then I will allow it simply because those that are not taking care of what I have provided for them will be taken care of, for it is said that we should love one another even as your father who is in heaven has loved you, so it's only right to do unto others the way you would like to be done unto. Treating others right will get a person a long way in life, only if we all believe.

How much scripture is God-breathed? As for this particular scripture, the worth of this scripture is God-breathed throughout the whole sixty-six books of the Bible from Genesis to Revelation. However, in this particular text, holy men of God were moved by his spirit to write inasmuch as being a willing vessel of God inspired to write down His words, which were and are good for teaching, leading, and guiding His people in the right direction.

It is also useful in the lives of His people to turn right and to go straight, that the man of God would be perfect and want for nothing, with patience, according to James 1:4. If you don't have patience, how can you be at peace, and without peace, how can you have any harmony? A time when this scripture was useful to me was when I just had to trust God at His word when I had no other choice but to believe and trust in Him. When I thought I was going to be taken away from my family, God stepped in and turned it around. There also was a time I had no other choice but to live on the street. He brought me through that situation, so then I never had to entertain myself as going hungry to a point of becoming like the prodigal son, but He delivered me.

The people or men of God were inspired by God to write His holy word, according to 2 Timothy 3:16, which were and is His book of heavenly and divine laws of God himself. God spoke through and worked with what He had made. Man is His vessel and used them of His own will that His word would tell the true story of what He wanted to happen in the lives of His people. Acts 2:4 (AV) tells us that "they were all filled with the Holy Ghost, and began to speak with other tongues as the Spirit gave them utterance."

In Exodus 34:27, God uses Moses and inspires him to write and speak to his people and to give them His laws, and the Lord says unto Moses, "Write thou these words: for after the tenor of these words I have made a covenant with thee and with Israel." So He told Moses to speak to his people. In the book of Jeremiah (1:5), Jeremiah was inspired by God's word. God told Jeremiah that He knew him even before he was formed in his mother's womb, and before he came forth out of her womb, He had sanctified him and ordained him for the people for the nation, so God let Jeremiah know that before he even existed, He knew him.

There is no hiding from God, no matter how you put it. He also inspired Hosea to do His will by way of a demonstration of how much He loves us, His people, despite us not acknowledging him as our God and despite us not walking with Him in His status. He is still waiting, willing, and ready to take us in and take us back from the enemy, as if nothing ever happened.

In the book of 2 Chronicles, God used the biggest word anyone could ever use. He said, "If my people, which are called by my name, shall humble themselves, and pray, and seek my face and turn from their wicked ways; then will I hear from heaven, and will forgive their sin, and will heal their land" (7:14 AV).Why do we have to have visual proof, in order for us to anything to get done, we have to do something? Well, Jesus came, worked, labored, suffered, and died for us. I do not think that anyone likes to eat uncooked food unless it's sushi or any of those other things that are eatable.

We are inspired by God's word in our dreams, according to Daniel 2:1, and Daniel 7:1 tells us that we receive His words by way of a vision. We are also inspired by God's word by just a touch from an inspired person or being of God. The Bible tells us that Daniel was touched by an angel of God while he was in a deep sleep, in which he had a vision in the form of a dream. In today's society, we might call it a déjà vu, but for Daniel, it was a real thing he had to deal with. Let's look at some of the real things that you deal with throughout the day and as the days go by. Well, one thing that we have to deal with is life and the fullness thereof. Life is so precious. God gave it to us, His people, to live in it and enjoy the fullness of it until the woman was beguiled and tricked of the enemy, the devil, Satan Slew Foot, and the Old Club Leg Snake, a viper of the generations to come. He tricked her into taking the forbidden fruit from out of the midst of the garden in which God told her not to even think about "for you will surely die." However, the enemy told her that she surely would not die; it's just the fact that God knows that "if you did eat, you would be as He is," knowing right from wrong. "I don't see anything wrong with that," she said, so because of that, we reap what we sow, we know good from evil, and now are our eyes open to know danger, fear, disrespect, honor, and dishonor.

It was not a sin until she gave it to Adam and he did eat, and so now it's a sin because the man did eat and not because he listened to the lesser vessel. The man is responsible for the woman and now also vice versa. Whatever goes on in the household is for the blame of the two, but mostly the man because he knows better and how to be the bigger person and take care of his woman like she ought to be taken care of, although it goes both ways. What's good for the goose is still also good for the gander, and it's all good. Prime example: without God, we can do nothing; without Him, we would fail; without God, we would be like a ship without a sail. It's just like the body without the spirit; it would only be a shell without a soul. So with all of that said, we need God in everything we do, and know that, if it was not for Him, we would not have awakened from our sleep.

Jesus's view of the Old Testament law/scripture was that the law is the law and is the law that is, and was in the times of old and that nothing changes, but He has come that the law would be fulfilled. For at the time, Moses, being a prophet of God who spread His word, was fully man and was destined to make an error, being born of a woman by the likes of a man, so then Jesus, being 100 percent man and 100 percent God in the flesh, is the only one who can fulfill His will, one that is without sin.

It is important to know the law to live by, according to God's word, if you want to be in good standing with God. He said to be or to love the world is to be enmity against Him. What does the fulfillment of prophecy prove about the Old Testament? Well, for one, it proves that according to Matthew 1:22–23; 4:14; 8:17; 12:17; 15:7–8, and 21:4–5, a virgin will be with a child, and we should call his name Emmanuel, which means "God with us," never to be alone again. Hey! I have to allow you to research for yourself.

Jesus came into the world and took our infirmities, suffered, and died for our sins for he cares for us, his little ones. Jesus is the one and only true son of God the almighty, in whom He is well pleased to send him for our sakes and that we, by His obedience, will accept him as our lord and savior and be saved? And that we have to beware of becoming hypocrites, saying things we ought not to say and doing things we ought not to do, going places we ought not to go, because the Bible says that these kinds draw close to Him or just when they are about to win, throw in the towel for they are only making sounds with their mouths, but their hearts are far from everything in Him and will say anything to get attention or someone to listen to them because it sounds good, which is not good for the soul.

The prediction of the New Testament by Jesus is that "I will go away for a little while, but I will send you back a comforter in my name, and if you forget whatsoever you have heard from and have forgotten he will bring it back to your remembrance would not be without." *He* meaning the comforter, also the spirit of truth, and to his followers, he said that because they have walked with him and have talked with him, traveled with him, they will be a witness in his stead. Jesus, who is being the author and the finisher of our faith, who for the joy that was set before him endured the cross, despising the shame, sits down at the right hand of the throne of God.

The difference of this book is that it gives instructions on how to prepare you and to protect that which stores information, that which tells the whole person, that which directs the whole person and protects that which remembers Him. For the word of God will come in the day to separate those who are not like Him, and it will separate thoughts from thoughts, and it will separate hearts from hearts that are like the mouths that say that it is, but hearts are far from what it says. Our attitudes toward the Bible should be sincere and directed in the position it should be daily as we study the word of God, and as we study the word of God, we should also take heed in what it is saying to us, and if we are confused, then we should seek an elder of the church, for he is then more connected at the present time than you are for the time being. The Bible states that if any among you are sick, don't get it all twisted now, because He also gave knowledge to the doctors to enable them. He performed the first surgery, when He cut Adam open to make Eve, by the taking of his ribs. Why did He take a rib and nothing else, and why just the ribs? My interpretation is that He took the rib of the man so that it would be her strength when the man was not around to carry her. It was taken for when she doesn't have anyone else to lean on; she will be able to stand on her own until the man of her dreams is able to help pull the heavy load, to pick her up, and to caress her when she needs a rub or when she need his strength that helps her recognize that she needs him, which is why it is not good for a man or a woman to do without each other, because in all reality, they really need each other more than they can imagine.

Why is it that we can believe that the wind, which we cannot see, is blowing when we see the effects of it, but we do not believe that God is real? Yes, it's true; we can't see Him, but the effects are real as He heals our bodies and takes us through the rain, the storms, and all types of problems. And we come out without the loss of anything that we needed, for He reached out to us, but we withdrew our hands as if it was away from Him and His help and as if we did not need Him. With Him being God, how do you think it feels when we reject Him and His love for us? We can also take the Bible at its word by way of seeing some of the things that it has predicted, such as those things that will be in the last days. For in the day of the Lord, we have to be strong in the grace of God, knowing that His grace is sufficient (2 Corinthians 12:9). We should meditate on His word day and night, observing to do His will and to concentrate on His word, knowing that it is the right thing to do, being doers of His words and not just hearers. Just hearing his word is not the same as studying and knowing for yourself. If we take God's word and hide it in our hearts, then we will have it for when the time comes when we can't find a Bible. We should always have it stored in our hearts so that when needed, as Jesus said, He will bring all things back to our remembrance. We should know that God's word is like a lamp unto our feet (Psalm 119:105) and is a light to our path.

Also, Proverbs 3:6 tells us that if we acknowledge Him as being God, He will direct our path. Also, the Bible tells us to trust in the Lord and not to lean on our own understanding. If we take heed to the word of God, according to what we have read and studied, if we stop jumping into everything that looks good to us, we will not keep on getting ourselves into trouble with others, ourselves, or God, because we are the only ones that can make things better or worse for ourselves. We allow someone else to do it for us, if we don't have the knowledge of direction in our lives. Then we are lots of our own free will because we did not seek, look, or ask for any help from anyone.

In our lifetimes, we have to know line upon line and precept upon precept, meaning that we have to know the commands of life and what they mean to us. We have to take them seriously and apply our very own walking and talking, meaning saying what you mean, and meaning what you say. A lot of times, we play games with other's lives and take them for what we think it should be like according to ourselves, and sometimes take people for granted and play with their lives, not realizing that the life you are playing with has feelings, and we don't expect any reaction to be negative; instead we laugh at how we used or so-called played with someone's mind, and think nothing of it, which is a crazy and stupid thing to do, because some are really in love. We just fail to believe it, and why is that? Is it because we really don't care or just don't give a crap about anybody or anything, and if that's so, then are we of the devil? Because that's the way he is; only if we knew, then we couldn't go wrong.

The Bible says that He will keep them in perfect peace, whose mind is stayed on Him, because he trusts in Him, according to Isaiah 26:3. Where is your mind if it is not on God? And where is your trust or who do you trust being that the Bible tells us to put our trust in no man? Who do you trust when things are not going your way or according to your plans? There is no one who is higher than God, and as some would say, that's your belief, and that's all we need to know, but if you don't read the Bible, how will you ever know? Let's put it like this. If you had not gone to school, would you have known what you know today? The answer is no, because everyone needs some kind of education, which is why everyone needs God and needs to study His word to show themselves approved. Amen.

Adoration and Appreciation

A woman is to be admired, appreciated, and touched. I am a strong believer of giving a woman everything I have when I am committed to her, because it's the proper thing to do, I think, and I expect to give a woman or my woman the pleasure she deserves, which is also the proper way of doing things to keep her. The Bible tells us that a woman is as precious as rubies. It also tells us in Proverbs 3:15 that she is more precious than rubies and is all of the things that a man can desire and cannot be compared to her. I am a strong believer of these sayings. How about you? And do you agree?

In Solomon 4:5, Solomon expresses the love he has for a woman. He tells us that she has two breasts that "are like fawns." They are the twins of a gazelle that feeds among the lilies. Talking about two breasts, in other words, they are exciting to be around and touch, squeeze, and use as pillows. Solomon goes on to say that women altogether are beautiful and a pleasure to have and to be around. (Song of Solomon 4)

In another instance, Solomon goes on to let us know that a woman will make your heart beat faster at just a glance into her eyes. He also said in the fourth chapter, verse nine that you have made my heart beat faster, my sister, my bride; you have made my heart beat faster with a single glance of your eyes, with a single strand of your hair. He goes on to adore her with his compliments to her, and he tells her that her lips drip honey; and that honey and milk are in and under her tongue.

My word to this is so, so sweet, sweet to the taste. I admire a woman for who she is and what she stands for, if, in fact, she is positive about what she does, the words she speaks, and the positivity she has toward her mom, because if she disrespects her mom, she will disrespect you and anyone who crosses her path. If a woman has respect for her mother and her mother has respect for her, then I know that I would have found a good, good woman indeed, simply because of her mother's happiness in life, because she stands and represents herself for other women, she knows what it takes to be a good woman and how to treat her man and not use him like a light switch or something with no life—in use for services when needed only.

A man will respect a woman more if she would just let him be the man and not her child who she thinks she has to raise again and again. A man will not be a man if he is led to believe that he's not because the woman thought she was picked up by a boy. Women say that they want good men, but what are they? Are you a good woman? If a woman or a man would just stop and listen to the verses, the question asked would be heard and answered. She and he would have a much better relationship with the other or that one of her or his dreams.

I have a daughter, and she is a very beautiful young lady. My daughter carries herself like a respectful young lady should carry herself when it comes to men trying to get with her, because she knows what they want. She knows what they are after because I told her from a man's point of view so that she would know, although there are times … well, I can't really say that because of how she makes me feel when she tries to mess with my nerves. I am so happy that she has grown up to be a very beautiful and respectful young lady who took after herself and nobody else because she knows who she is, as well as what she does not want to be.

My daughter is her own person with her own traits and personality. Although she did get something from me and her mother, she has my looks, but she didn't until that moment came when I found out that she did have something that her mother had and that's when you get on her nerves, then she falls into a protective mode in order to maintain her composure, and when she gets like that with me, then the time has come to call it a day. See you later. Love you. Because it's when her eyes start to wink, that means it's time to go. And that's the way I think it should be when you start to get upset with your significant other. Then it's time to vacate, not her/him but the problem that can eventually separate the two of you, which is called knowing when to just shut up and let bygones be bygones. Two people hollering at each other cannot hear what the other one is saying because everybody wants to be heard but never wants to listen.

When my daughter allows herself to be in a protective mode and we are together, it reminds me of her mother when she is having a bad day in which the "enemy" in that appears smaller than anything or anybody and is kind and very nice to be around. But when you get on her nerves or sometimes you don't have to get on her nerves to pull her strings—it could be that she is having a bad day—then she takes it out on whoever is around her and gives that person a bad day, if they would just only listen to her, although I think that her anger comes from her being so short and wanting to be tall. That is not happening as she knows, so then she becomes the meanest person anyone would ever not want to be around, and I truly think that because some people are short, it has a ripple effect on their emotions.

When a man loves a woman—I mean really loves her—when he loves her, he would do anything and everything for her, more than you can imagine, and it literally goes to his head. He starts daydreaming and seeing himself in the future with her. I mean he starts to breathing hard, his heart starts to pumping fast, and most of the time, he does not know how to approach a woman who he really wants to get to know. He tries and tries to please his woman every chance he gets. There is only one thing that gets in a man's way, and that is the very person that he sticks his chest out for and tries to please but is let down . A man will go out of his way to make sure that he does what he has to do in order to please his woman, but the woman has to put herself out of the way, meaning she has to stop having crazy thoughts and telling him what a man is supposed to be like when she has never been with one before in her life.

A woman is the pride of a man's life and the joy in the center of it. It has been that way since the devil was kicked out of heaven, so then the man, if he has it to give, will give his woman the stars, the birds, and the trees. I believe he would give her even the moon, the sun, and everything beneath and above his throne. Samson played around and played around and Delilah played around with him until she broke him down, and it caused him to lose his strength, his eyesight, and his unwillingness to stand for what he was supposed to be standing for. Without a chief who can lead? And without a follower, then who can take advice and learn from it?

Definitions of Things That Happen in Relationships

Come now—"Come now, and let us reason together, saith the LORD: though your sins be as scarlet, they shall be as white as snow; though they are red like crimson, they shall be as wool" (Isaiah 1:18 AV). Whenever and wherever there is an agreement, there is peace. Though you might not agree, agree that you disagree and do not carry on with the same old thing.

Dog—Any animal belonging to the same family, a domesticated carnivore, one that refrains from action that would alter an existing problem or create a new one; when a problem arise, there is no need to get an attitude to try an solve an unsolvable situation, on to the next one. Paul said it is better to live in a corner of the housetop, than with a brawling woman in a wide house.(Proverbs 21:9) In other words, the man that has been hurt, has now turned to his own vomit you created. (Proverbs 26:11). (AV)

Do things—Refer "to do things that cause a reaction." Retaliation is irresponsible. To do things is to get away from things that cause negativity in the home, on the job, and or even when alone, even while in your peacefulness.

Family wrecker—John 10:10 (AV)—"The thief cometh not, but for to steal, and to kill, and to destroy: I am come that they might have life, and that they might have it more abundantly." Whatever it was that caught your eyes when you first met, the other set of eyes is still there, and the only reason why it's not there is because somebody has been hoodwinked, blindfolded, and does not recognize that what was there is still there, and the grass is truly not greener on the other side.

The Sower—Mark 4:4: Some fell by the wayside and were devoured. Some fell on stony ground and had no power to live but died, and there were some that fell, and some fell in the fire and were scorched because it had no covering and withered away. But then there were those that fell on good ground that sprang up, went forth, prospered, and were reliable, which were the ones that always were there but were not fed, were not nurtured, and were not paid any attention to, ignored, neglected, abused, talked about, and were not respected anymore as before. Be not forgetful to entertain strangers: for thereby some have entertained angels and did not know of it.

Haters—Refer to **family wrecker.** Haters are those who hate just to hate and don't know why they hate. Haters are those that hate you for just being you because of who you are and, not only that, but because of whose you are. It's God or the other. It does not matter to the hater and the other. The only reason why hate flows so deeply in their hearts is because they are lacking love.

I need some time—An invasion has occurred and is about to take place, take over, and make predictions, decisions, and provisions that will take over, if it is not caught in time, before it takes over the mind. It ties in with house wrecker, which is an intruder, in a rodent way. It makes one feel like one doesn't need what's before him or her anymore, and the beat goes on, a term we are all familiar with.

Hell—Isaiah 5:14 (AV): "Therefore hell hath enlarged herself and opened **her** mouth without measure: and their glory, and their multitude, and their splendor, and he that rejoices, shall descend into it." Any time there is a disagreement, discouragement, discomfort, disrespect, or anything that is not right or is not going right in the home, at the job, with your so-called friend, or even with yourself, knows that you are being drawn to its attention. It's like a gravity pull or a suck hole or a whirlwind, pulling you away from that which is good.

For better or worst—It's never better before, but it is better afterward. You cannot think in the past when you are trying to go forward. It is never better when you have dirty laundry until you wash it, because now it's clean, and when it is clean, keep it clean because you are never recovering. It is a continuous process. It is never ending, but when you have recovered, and then you are complete.

Men with men—Romans 1:27 tells us that men, instead of having normal sexual relations with women, burn with lust for each other, doing shameful things with other men, and as a result of this sin, they suffered within themselves the penalty of death. Most likely, they are those pretty boys, doing things on the down low; hoping that what they are doing will never come to the light, stuck in the closet, which is another reason why hell has enlarged **herself**.

Vile affections—For the same reason, because of vile affections, women did change the natural use of that which is against nature and God, so He gave them up to a reprobate mind, which means he rejected them.

One flesh—Mark 10:8 (New International Version): "And the two will become one flesh.' So they are no longer two, but one flesh." This means when you hurt, I feel it; when you cry, I feel it; when you are in agony, I feel it; and when you are going through something that seems impossible, I should not run from it but stand up to it, because when two agree, what can separate the two? God said He would never leave us nor forsake us, and we don't have to beg for anything if our minds are kept on him. Amen. Which means it is so.

Worship—John 4:24 (AV): "God *is* a Spirit: and they that worship him must worship *him* in spirit and in truth."

"Thou shalt not make unto thee any graven image, or any likeness *of any thing* that *is* in heaven above, or that *is* in the earth beneath, or that is in the water under the earth: Thou shalt not bow down thyself to them, nor serve them: for I the LORD thy God *am* a jealous God, visiting of the fathers upon the children unto the third and fourth generation of them that hate me; And showing mercy unto thousands of them that love me, and keep my commandments" (Exodus 20:4–6 AV).

Pretty boys—There are no bodies prettier than the man or woman you have met that was not pretty before. In other words, he or she is the same person who was adored and admired before; it's just a refusal to see what's real, hoodwinked, but made to see different from and by the other source, who is the enemy.

Good soil—"Be not deceived; God is not mocked: for whatsoever a man soweth, that shall he also reap. (For example, if you plant a tomato, you will get a tomato. That shall you also reap.) For he that soweth to his flesh shall of the flesh reap corruption; but he that sows to the Spirit shall of the Spirit reap life everlasting" (Galatians 6:7–8 AV).

Whenever you plant or invest in something, you should check it out first so that you will know who, what, and when to invest. If you are going out on a date with someone, you should check the soil out and make sure you are planting your goods in rich soil, soil that has a need and not a want. Otherwise, if you plant your goods in any other soil, like the clay we walk on, you would be planting in places where nothing ever grows. If you are planting in negative grounds that do not know how to yield, then you are planting in a blank field. If you plant on stony grounds, you cannot make alive what's dead, for you are not Jesus. In other words, you can't change what's already arranged.

The root of it all is, if there is no root, there is no life, and if there is no life, there is no spirit. God said that those that worship Him must worship Him in spirit and in truth. If there are no grounds in which you planted, there will be no life yielded up, because it has no ground and root of itself. It has no substance and cannot be trusted; it will drain out everything you have or ever had. Philippians 3:2 tells us to watch them dogs, beware of workers, and beware of the concision. It will send you to a place not made for man, but for the devil and his demons only.

It is very important to live your life according to the will of God, but some will ask questions. What is God's will for me and in my life? The answer to that is trust God and do good, so shall thou dwell in the land and verily thou shall be fed. Psalm 37:3 and Proverbs 5:5–6 tell us to trust in the Lord with all of our hearts and for us not to lean on our own understanding, and in all of our ways acknowledge Him, as He will make your paths straight and direct them as well. Sometimes we need direction in our lives, needless to say, all the daylong if we are not careful of the things we do and the things we say to others, even to ourselves. It can cause a person to fall right into the trap of illusion fixed and mixed imagination, thinking that we should be here when we should be there, wherever here or there may be. First Corinthians 15:33 (AV) says, "Be not deceived: evil communication corrupts good manners." If you are in a relationship and you develop bad manners or already have them but didn't allow them only to come out when tested or tempted, then you have bad manners that will corrupt not only the one you love but also a whole nation. First, we have to keep ourselves in check before we can put or attempt to put someone else in check. Anything other than that is being a hypocrite. Are you a hypocrite?

Whenever one finger is pointing at you, several others are pointing right back. Matthew 7:5 (NLT) explains, "Hypocrite! First get rid of the log in your own eye; then you will see well enough to deal with the speck in your friend's eye." In other words, don't cast the blame on anybody else until you check yourself.

Things to Look For when Entering into "A" Relationship

1. Whenever entering into a relationship, you should always be cautious. Just like there are antichrists, there are anti-relationships as well. Sometimes, thoughts arrive from out of nowhere, but somehow end up in the heads of the pursuer, in whom there are already dreams of the imagination and of lust that have manifested, because of an imagination. Second Samuel 11:5 says that one day King David decided to take a walk around his palace. During his walk, he saw a woman bathing in a "purification state of being," and because of what he'd imagined and seen in his head, he decided to send for her. And because of who he was, she came to him, and they did sleep together. And as they did, they begat Solomon, who would also become a king much later on in the story. Long story short, he betrayed his "boy," and she betrayed her husband, "Uriah the Hittite." (2 Samuel 11-12) (NKJV).

Desires are good, but for the right reasons, not for lustful feelings sitting in your heart. If that was the case, you could only look at it as a power struggle. If it's not your way, there's no other way. What a selfish thought! For instance, and first of all and far most, in the beginning, you are strangers seeking the energy of another in order to get to know each other; at some point, you feel that you're attracted one to another because of an energy called gut feelings, which nine times out of ten are going to be true, whether it's good or bad. However, some emotional feelings, which are in most cases, are just feelings loneliness that give rise to a desire to taste or try it. You might like it, but what if you don't like it? Then what?

Everything that looks good does not mean it is. Wanting to try a piece of cake because of the frosting and what it stands for or what's in it as you know what should be in it does not mean that it is; it's plastic or make-believe. It's not Coca-Cola. It's not "the real thing." Women and men are just alike in most cases and situations, yet are afraid to admit it. You should always learn of each other and of each other's background. Check out what kind of a background you are about to get yourself involved in. Straight to the point, there might be unknown health problems or financial problems. Hey, you never know, but you, at least, want to be ready for it. There might even be mental problems, jealousy problems, I'm-the-boss problems, "uncompromising" problems, what-I-say-goes problems, and just plain old shut-up-I'm-talking problems. You might not want to put yourself (and if there's children) then you as a responsible person, have to be very careful.

2. Close encounters: When getting closer, the opposite sex should be the only thing you should be attracted to. The Bible reminds us of what He has done before and what He is about to do. "God said let us make mankind in our image, in our likeness, so that they may rule over the fish in the sea and the birds in the sky, over the livestock and over all the wild animals, and over all the creatures that move along the ground." So God created mankind in His own image; in the image of God, He created them; male and female, He created he them. In the *A* clause of verse 28, God blessed them and said to them, "Be fruitful and increase in number, fill the earth and subdue it."

The one person you want to share a part of your life with should not be complicated, arranged, or difficult; neither should that person be simple. However, he or she can be a challenge. Why a challenge? Well, if the eagle didn't force her eaglets out of the nest, they would have never learned how to fly. Every now and then, in order for someone to be pleased with us, we have to do extraordinary things to please each other that are sometime self-challenging. Life is not about just giving, giving, and giving, more and more, but it's about returns as well; it's not always going to be fifty-fifty. There will be some seventy-thirty, some sixty-forty, whatever it takes. But it should never be about who is doing the most or about who is not, for better or for worst, even what's not agreed upon sometimes. I don't agree to, even a boyfriend/girlfriend relationship, as well because it can lead into marriage, and if it does, then what? You will already know the difference and how to deal with situations that may come or arrive in your lives. From my perspective, there should be a yearning for each other yet respect one another's wishes, dreams, and desires.

Sometimes when getting to know a person you are truly interested in, you have to be willing to take a risk and or a chance, and after all, we take chances every day; however, most of them are unknown, and some of them are known, yet we challenge it anyway, thinking in our heads that maybe it's not as it seems, and we end up fooling ourselves. Whichever way you look at it, it's still a chance. Some chances we take in our lives—for instance getting into a cab, going out on the very first date with someone we are trying to get to know, invitations to dinner not knowing where you're going or headed or who's preparing it." We go to movies not knowing who is in the movies.

We seldom would go on trips, to ball games, or out on other outings and so forth. Then finally, we meet the parents, go over the dos and don'ts. In some cases, some of us have one, while others have both, whichever way it goes, it has to or should be done. In my opinion, there is a proper way to introduce your now better half or your significant other so that things can now be stabilized, so that your parents or parent can get a feel of what you are getting yourself into, because they normally are able to miraculously see things you have not seen as of yet. You might not think so, but it's true.

Sometimes we can get caught up in things that feel good to us, but in most cases, they are not good for us. It's just a feeling, but they are not true feelings; true feelings come from within, from the heart and not the chest, feet, eyes, or any parts of the body, other than the heart, for that is where true love resides. First Corinthians 13:4–8: "Love is patient, love is kind. It does not envy, it does not boast, it is not proud. It does not dishonor others, it is not self-seeking, it is not easily angered, and it keeps no records of wrongs. Love does not delight in evil but rejoices with the truth. It always protects, always trusts, always hopes, and always perseveres. Love never fails, but where there are prophecies, they will cease; where there are tongues, they will be still; where there is knowledge, it will pass away" (NIV).

If these things are followed and are thought upon, you can never go wrong. Don't give in to anything else other than these, for it is the way and the word of God, for God is love all by himself, according to 1 John 4:8 (NIV) says whoever does not love does not know God, because God is love. Know God. Be of Him and let Him be the greater one in your life, and everything else will fall into place; however, be equally yoked together and not unequally because it will not work, and be of the same faith, for as God loved the church so ought we to love each other. As God gives us strength, knowledge, wisdom, and understanding to be able to understand each other's verses, downsizing; because something went wrong, fix it not by yourself but together. If a house be divided, it cannot and will not stand, together or apart, but definitely not apart.

3. Mingling time: To mix or bring together in combination, usually without the loss of individual characteristics. So now as the mind starts to wonder and you start seeing yourselves together, it might just be you two. In these days and times, there are a lot of dropout parents who are now in the picture, and there are a lot of step-in parents who have found their way or have had no other choices in life but to give in to what has already been created. With readymade families, you have to realize that even in this, you are taking a chance with your children and your significant other's children; however, it primarily is going to be a chance we all will have to take some day, if we want to be, at least, partially happy.

As long as we can put two and two together and get four, everything will add up to what it's supposed to be, no more and no less. Togetherness as a family is very important, for it was the family first, then the church, and so now you want to start a family, but in order to start a family, you would have to be well adjusted for the modifications of a life-changing experience and the impact that it will cause in those lives. It is amazing what two can accomplish when two heads are thinking alike together. Sometimes you have to agree, even though you disagree; it will keep the peace in your lives and your homes. If your head does not start to swell, be of one accord and of one mind with each other and definitely with no secrets kept from each other unless it's for a good surprise for pleasing and not displeasing or displeasure. For example, if your neck didn't work, your head would not be able to turn from your wicked ways and let God have His way in your life. Never should we ever put anything before God, not even ourselves. We shouldn't allow anybody to cause us to turn against each other; that is a destroyer of any relationship. Always let your yea be a yea, and you nay be nay or else something will come in and cause confusion in your household, family, relationships, and in your lives for God, and you are not the author of confusion if you are of Him.

4. So now you're in a stage of life and have started seeing the good as well as the bad about each other, the likes and dislikes, whereas they were not there before, and why is that? Now that the relationship has done the impossible, the people who already thought it wasn't going to last are knocking at your door. The devil is mad because it's lasting, and now it's tempting time; it's time to see if you're true to yourself and to your significant other, and now he is going to try and tear it apart because it is ordained of God; whereas if it was not and as long as you stayed in it, that would be all right with him. For as much as you haven't said I do, or I will, he is pleased with it.

Have you ever noticed married people before they got married? And now that their marriage is lasting and they are happy, it puts a frown on his face, but he will encourage a ungodly relationship to stay together, encourage, and pound on it to break up, have his imps calling you, telling you things that needs not to be heard of, or even thought of, because, nine times out of ten, it is too negative to hear or digest. Let those kinds keep to themselves. They are called truce breakers. Second Timothy 3:3–5 tells us that they are without natural affection, truce breakers, false accusers, and incontinent, fierce, despisers of those that are good; traitors, reckless, conceited lovers of pleasure more than lovers of God. People that have a form of godliness will deny the power thereof. From such, turn away. The main thing to not do is never let anything negative come into your lives, the man or the woman. No matter what, put a lid on it, seal it, and throw it away, and when you throw it away, do it in Jesus's name, amen, and may God continue blessing relationships until the next time. Praise the name of the Lord.

Mark 10:9 (NIV): "Let no one split apart what God has joined together." That means mama, daddy, sister, brother, aunt, uncle, first cousin, second cousins, or third cousins, not even grandparents can separate you as God has joined or brought you together; however, make sure that it was God who brought you together. If it's man and man or woman and woman, know this, and that is, it was not God's doing for He made the woman for the man alone. Don't get it twisted; it's not the other way around, and if it was so, then he would have told the same sex to multiply, but he didn't, and being that he didn't and you do, it is a slap in God's face.

Romans 6:23: "For the wages of sin is death, but the gift of God is eternal life." So please, for your soul's sake, don't think that God is not watching, for if He watches the sparrow, you should know that he watches you because His eyes never closes, only ours, so that He can watch over us as we sleep and slumber through the night. God is good all the time and has never failed at anything. He is your keeper, supplier, healer, savior, the door, the way, and redeemer until He calls us to stand in the line of judgment. The love of God is with us always, no matter what. Hebrews 13:5 (CSB Holman Bible) states, "Your life should be free from the love of money." Be satisfied with what you have. For he himself has said, "I will never leave you or forsake you." Therefore, we may boldly say that the Lord is my helper; I will not be afraid. What can man do to me? Praise the Lord, and I hope that the information I have shared with you will help rebuild, establish, keep together, or reconcile your relationships. In Jesus's name. Amen. If you have any questions I can be reached at via email Loced1@live.com orWorthshipgod@yahoo.com. Peace, love and happiness: God loves you and so do I.

About the Author

I believe I am qualified to write my book because I think people really need to hear my side of the story when it comes to broken relationships.

I had some good times and I had some hills to climb, and sometimes I have to ask a question and that is why there was so much pain and questions like: Why did it have to happen to me? I live in Syracuse, New York, and have been since 1985. I am an ordained minister as well as a business owner. I have three boys and a daughter, and I love all of them the same.

Printed in the United States
By Bookmasters